OVER 100 FAST & FURIOUS TIMESAVING

Quick & Easy Grilling

BEEF AND LAMB • ZESTY BEEF BRISKET • TEXAS BRISKET • TERIYAKI CHUCK ROAST • BARBECUED ROA • PATIO POT ROAST

CAJUN ROAST TENDERLOIN • CHUCK WAGON PEPPER STEAK • PARTY STEAK DIANE • ONION-BUTTERED SIRLOIN • GRILLED PEPPERED STEAK

WITH MAPLE CIDER GLAZE • BAR UED STRIP AK • CARNE ASADA • HONEY-GRILLE STEAKS AND ONIONS • SESAME FLANK STEAK

FLANK STEAK NOVA SCOTIA • S LOIN MUSHROOMS • KABOB OVER ALS • B D BEEF KABOBS • STEAK FAJITAS

BARBECUED SHORT RIBS • TORPE URGER • SPIC AM URGE NESIAN • HA ERS ON THE GRILL • CHARCOALED MEAT LOAF

POOR MAN'S FILETS MIGNON • ME IN-A-BUNDLE RILL MEAL ONE C DOGS • N ABOBS • LAMB CHOPS INDONESIAN SATAY

LAMB SHISH KABOBS • ORIENTAL GRILL PORK C ORK ERLOIN • ORIENTAL PORK TENDERLOIN

LAYERED PORK MEDALLIONS AND SLAW • SOUTHWESTERN-STUFFED PORK RLOIN • JAMAICAN PORK TENDERLOIN • GRILLED PORK SANDWICH

PORK LOIN ROAST A L'ORANGE • PORK AND CHICKEN FAJITAS • ORI TAL PORK KABOBS • INDONESIAN PORK • PORK AND VEGETABLE SHISH

KABOBS • VIETNAMESE SKEWERED PORK BROCHETTE • BARBECUED P EAR ORK STEAK BUNDLES • CRANBERRY-GLAZED PORK ROAST

DRY-RUB BARBECUE PORK • BOSTON BUTT ROAST • SMOKED RIB WITH NEY STARD SAUCE • FANTASTIC RIBS • HAWAIIAN HAM STEAKS

HAM STEAK WITH ENGLISH CUMBERLAND SAUCE • CHICKEN BRE S SUPREM • GRILLED CURRIED CHICKEN • GRAPEFRUIT CHICKEN BREASTS

LEMON PEPPER CHICKEN • GRILLED CHICKEN PIZZA GRI KEN • PEPPERED CHICKEN BREASTS WITH ROSEMARY AND GARLIC

JAMAICA JERK WAR EAGLES • LEMON-LIME ILLING ICKEN • CHICKEN WITH ASPARAGUS • GRILLED RASPBERRY MUSTARD CHICKEN

MUSTARD PEPPER CHICKEN WITH HERB SAUCE • CRANBERR AZED C ICKEN HALVES • ALOHA GRILLED CHICKEN AND

PINEAPPLE KABOBS • CHICKEN TENDER KAB BACON CKEN USHRO KABOBS • SURF AND TURF KABOBS • GRILLED

CHICKEN AND SAUCE • LEMON-LIME SPAR G CHICKEN CHICKEN ARRAGON DIJON CHICKEN • 24-HOUR CHICKEN

LIME AND HOT PEPPER CHICKEN • GRILLED TURKEY BREAST • SMOKED RKEY RILLED TUR EY TENDERLOIN • GRILLED WHOLE TURKEY WITH LIME

SPICY TURKEY FAJITAS • TY • TURKEY AR FISH • BLACKENED REDFISH • GRILLED FISH WITH

BANANA SAUCE • GRILL MAHIMAHI • GRILLED MAHIMAHI IN RED N • SALMON BURGERS • GRILLED SALMON WITH BASIL MUSTARD

CRUST • SMOKED ALA N SALMON • GRILLE YONNAI • GRILLE ALM STEAK • GRILLED HALIBUT KABOBS

GRILLED TROUT IN FOIL • ACON-STUFFED OUT ORIENTA RILL UNA EAKS • ZEST RILLED UNA • GRILL TUNA WITH MUSTARD MARINADE

TUNA BURGERS WITH SESA AYONNAISE • SW DFISH WI RED P SAUCE • GR ED SCA OPS • GARLIC BUTTER • GRILLED SHRIMP-

ON-A-STICK • SHRIMP FAJITAS • AGIN' CAJUN SHRIMP • BARBECU SHRIMP • SHRIMP AND ORE S • CLAM BAKE IN FOIL

GRILLED CHEESE BREAD • BEEF JERKY • HICKORY-SMOKED BACON ED PINEAPPLE CHUNKS • CON-WRA ED BANANAS • PARMESAN

CHICKEN STRIPS • SESAME CHICKEN FINGERS • GRILLED P GREEN BEANS AND RED ONION • MANGO, SWEET PEPPER AND

GRILLED RED ONION SALAD • GRILLED EGGPLANT SALAD BEEF SALAD • SIRLOIN STEAK SALAD • GRILLED CHICKEN

AND RED PEPPER PASTA SALAD • CHICKEN SALAD WITH D CHICKEN CAESAR SALAD • WARM LENTIL AND GRILLED

SALMON SALAD • ZESTY HORSERADISH CORN ON THE COB • GRILLED EGGPLANT AND SQUASH • ITALIAN EGGPLANT

CASSEROLE • GRILLED MUSHROOMS WITH BACON • GRI ROOMS • HONEY-BAKED ONIONS • BARBECUED ONIONS

DILLY TATERS • POTATOES-ON-A-STICK • GRILLED NEW PO TO CASSEROLE • GINGERED ACORN SQUASH • JIFFY TOMATO STACK-UPS

BROILED TOMATOES • GRILLED ZUCCHINI • GRILLED TATOUILLE • GRILLED VEGETABLE KABOBS • FOIL-GRILLED VEGETABLES

FRUIT KABOBS ON THE GRILL • GRILLED PEAR AND BANANA KABOBS • C AMELIZED APRICOT APPLE KABOBS • BARBECUED APPLES

BANANAS FOSTER ON THE GRILL • GRILLED BANANA SPL • GRILLED PEAC S FLAMBE • GRILLED PEACHES WITH RASPBERRY PUREE

HONEY-GRILLED PEACHES • GRILLED PINEAPPLE • PARA SE GRILLED APAYA • G ILLED S'MORES • GRILLED MAHIMAHI IN RED ONION BUTTER

GRILLED TROUT IN FOIL • BACON-STUFFED TROUT • ORIENTAL GRILLED TUNA STEAKS • ZESTY GRILLED TUNA • GRILLED TUNA WITH MUSTARD MARINADE

President: Thomas F. McDow III

Vice-President: Dave Kempf

Managing Editor: Mary Cummings

Project Editor: Anne Lacy Boswell

Art Director: Steve Newman

Book Design: David Malone

Typographers: Jessie Anglin, Sara Anglin

Production Coordinator: Powell Ropp

This cookbook is a collection of our favorite recipes,

which are not necessarily original recipes.

Published by

Favorite Recipes® Press

an imprint of

FRP

P.O. Box 305142

Nashville, TN 37230

1-800-358-0560

Manufactured in the United States of America

First Printing 2003 30,000 copies

Quick & Easy Grilling

CONTENTS

Quick & Easy Grilling

INTRODUCTION

Cooking outdoors has never been easier or more fun. Grilling seems to bring out the best flavor in everything, and it is not just for summer anymore! Bring the taste of warm weather to cold weather meals with Patio Pot Roast or how about Grilled Turkey Breast? Grilling is not just for burgers anymore either. We have included new dishes sure to be your favorites, such as Salmon with Tarragon Mayonnaise and Grapefruit Chicken Breasts. Try an elegant grilled dish such as Grilled Cranberry-Glazed Pork for a candlelight dinner for two, or invite a bunch over to watch the big game and serve something as casual as Zesty Beef Brisket. Begin your meal with an appetizer or a salad from the grill, such as Grilled Potato Salad, and then finish it off with a grilled dessert, such as Bananas Foster on the Grill. Whatever the occasion, these recipes are sure to earn a spot on your grill.

Quick & Easy Grilling

FIRE UP THE GRILL

- Start charcoal fire with bed of briquets 2 to 3 inches deep about 30 to 40 minutes before cooking. Make your own fire starters by placing briquets in egg cartons. Pour melted paraffin over briquets. Place on top of unlighted briquets.

- Heat coals to the specified temperature.
  Very Hot (450°) . . Coals will be glowing with gray ash on edges.
  Hot (400°) . . . . . . Coals will be covered with gray ash. You will be able to hold your hand 4 inches from heat source for 2 seconds.
  Medium (350°) . . You will be able to hold your hand 4 inches from heat source for 4 seconds.
  Low (300°) . . . . . You will be able to hold your hand 4 inches from heat source for 5 seconds.

Marinating Tips

- Sprinkle salt over the meat before marinating to ensure that the food is seasoned evenly. While the food is marinating, turn it once or twice to make sure that all surfaces are saturated.

- Allow for 1/2 to 3/4 cup of marinade for every 1 pound of food.

- Always marinate in the refrigerator using a glass, stainless-steel, or plastic container. Use a container just large enough for the food or a sealable plastic bag.

- Do not reuse the marinade once it has come in contact with raw meat, poultry, or fish. If you plan to use it for basting or as part of a sauce, bring it to a boil to kill any harmful bacteria from the raw food.

Quick & Easy Grilling

GRILLING FROM THE GARDEN

Any vegetable or fruit can be grilled in foil packets. However, most vegetables and fruits can be placed directly on the grill. Rinse, trim, and precook vegetables if necessary. Brush with olive oil or melted margarine. Cook over medium coals until slightly charred and tender.

Use grilled vegetables as an addition to pasta salads, to top pizza or hamburgers, to stir into cooked vegetables or baked beans, and to spice up spaghetti sauce, sandwiches, or pitas. Served grilled fruit alone or with vanilla ice cream or as an addition to baked desserts or casseroles.

Timing for Grilled Vegetables and Fruits

	Preparation	Precooking time	Grilling time
Apples	Cut into halves.	Do not precook	4 to 6 minutes
Asparagus	Snap off and discard tough bases of stems.	3 to 4 minutes	3 to 5 minutes
Bananas	Peel; cut into halves lengthwise.	Do not precook	4 minutes
Bell peppers	Remove stem. Cut into quarters; cut into 1-inch-wide strips.	Do not precook	8 to 10 minutes
Corn	Leave husks on.	Do not precook	15 to 20 minutes
Peaches	Remove pit. Cut into halves.	Do not precook	4 to 5 minutes
Pineapple	Peel and core. Cut into 1/4-inch slices.	Do not precook	3 to 5 minutes
Summer squash and zucchini	Rinse; cut off ends. Quarter lengthwise into long strips.	Do not precook	5 to 6 minutes
Tomatoes	Cut into quarters.	Do not precook	20 minutes

Quick & Easy Grilling

Mainstream Meats

Zesty Beef Brisket

1 (3- to 5-pound) beef brisket
2 teaspoons salt
1/4 teaspoon pepper
1 medium onion, sliced
1/2 cup ketchup
2 tablespoons light brown sugar
1 tablespoon Worcestershire
   sauce
1 teaspoon instant coffee
   granules

Combine brisket with enough water to cover in large heavy saucepan. Add salt, pepper and onion. Simmer, covered, for 3 hours or until tender; drain. Combine ketchup, brown sugar, Worcestershire sauce and coffee granules in bowl; mix well. Baste brisket with sauce. Grill over medium-hot coals for 15 to 20 minutes or until browned, turning and basting often with sauce.

Yield: 8 servings

Texas Brisket

Garlic powder to taste
Salt and pepper to taste
Paprika to taste
Chili powder to taste
1 large beef brisket
1 cup vinegar
1/2 cup vegetable oil
1/3 cup Worcestershire sauce
1/4 cup water
1/4 cup lemon juice
1 1/2 teaspoons salt
1 1/2 teaspoons paprika
1 1/2 teaspoons hot pepper sauce
1 teaspoon garlic powder
1 teaspoon chili powder
3 bay leaves

Combine garlic powder, salt, pepper, paprika and chili powder to taste in bowl; mix well. Rub over the brisket. Cover and let stand at room temperature for 1 hour. Combine vinegar, oil, Worcestershire sauce, water, lemon juice, 1 1/2 teaspoons each salt, paprika and hot pepper sauce, 1 teaspoon each garlic powder and chili powder and bay leaves in saucepan; simmer for 15 minutes. Grill brisket over medium-hot coals for 2 to 4 hours or to desired degree of doneness, turning and basting often with sauce.

Yield: 8 servings

Quick & Easy Grilling

Teriyaki Chuck Roast

1 1/2 teaspoons meat tenderizer
2 pounds boneless chuck roast
1/4 cup soy sauce
1 tablespoon vegetable oil
2 tablespoons water
3 tablespoons brown sugar
3 garlic cloves, minced
1/2 teaspoon ginger
1 tablespoon honey
1/2 teaspoon salt
1/2 teaspoon pepper

Sprinkle meat tenderizer over roast in shallow dish. Refrigerate, covered, overnight. Combine soy sauce, oil, water, brown sugar, garlic, ginger, honey, salt and pepper in bowl; mix well. Pour over roast. Marinate, covered, in refrigerator for 1 to 2 days, turning occasionally; drain. Grill over hot coals to desired degree of doneness.

Yield: 6 servings

Patio Pot Roast

1 (3- to 4-pound) blade-bone
    pot roast, 1 1/2 to 2 inches
    thick
Salt and pepper to taste
1/2 cup ketchup
3 tablespoons flour
1 tablespoon light brown sugar
1 tablespoon Worcestershire
    sauce
1 tablespoon vinegar
1/2 teaspoon dry mustard
Vegetables such as carrots,
    celery and onions, sliced

Brown roast on grill over medium-hot coals for 30 minutes. Season with salt and pepper. Combine ketchup, flour, brown sugar, Worcestershire sauce, vinegar and dry mustard in bowl; mix well. Spoon half the sauce in center of large piece of heavy-duty foil. Place roast on top of sauce. Top with vegetables; add remaining sauce. Fold foil to enclose and seal edges. Place on another piece of foil on grill. Grill over medium-hot coals for 1 1/2 to 2 hours or to desired degree of doneness.

Yield: 8 servings

Quick & Easy Grilling

Barbecued Roast and Vegetables

2 tablespoons butter or
  margarine
1 onion, chopped
1/2 cup chopped celery
1 cup ketchup
3/4 cup water
2 tablespoons vinegar
2 tablespoons lemon juice
2 tablespoons Worcestershire
  sauce
2 tablespoons light brown sugar
1 teaspoon dry mustard
1 teaspoon salt
1/4 teaspoon pepper
1 (4-pound) eye-of-round roast
Vegetables such as potatoes,
  green bell peppers,
  mushrooms and carrots

Melt butter in saucepan over medium-high heat.
Add onion and celery and cook until tender, stirring
occasionally. Add ketchup, water, vinegar, lemon
juice, Worcestershire sauce, brown sugar, dry mustard,
salt and pepper; mix well. Reduce heat and simmer
for 15 minutes. Grill roast over medium-hot coals for
20 minutes or until brown, turning occasionally. Cut
vegetables into 1-inch pieces. Place roast in large pan.
Add sauce; arrange vegetables around roast. Cover
and grill over medium-hot coals for 1 1/2 to 2 hours
or to desired degree of doneness.

Yield: 8 servings

Cajun Tenderloin

1 (4-pound) beef tenderloin
6 garlic cloves, sliced
3 jalapeño chiles, sliced
1 bunch scallions, sliced
Salt, pepper and cayenne
  pepper to taste

Cut slits in tenderloin. Insert garlic, jalapeño chiles
and scallions into slits. Rub with salt, pepper and
cayenne pepper. Grill over medium coals for 1 to
1 1/2 hours or to desired degree of doneness, turning
frequently. May substitute bell pepper strips for
jalapeño chiles if desired.

Yield: 8 servings

Quick & Easy Grilling

Chuck Wagon Pepper Steak

1 (3-pound) round steak,
    2 inches thick
2 teaspoons unseasoned meat
    tenderizer
1 cup wine vinegar
1/2 cup vegetable or olive oil
3 tablespoons lemon juice
2 tablespoons instant minced
    onion
2 teaspoons thyme
1 teaspoon marjoram
1 bay leaf
1/4 cup peppercorns, crushed

Rub steak evenly on both sides with tenderizer. Pierce deeply in several places with fork; place in shallow pan. Combine vinegar, oil, lemon juice, minced onion, thyme, marjoram and bay leaf in bowl; mix well. Pour over and around roast. Let stand, covered, at room temperature for 1 to 2 hours, turning every 30 minutes; drain. Pound half the peppercorns into each side with wooden mallet. Grill 6 inches above hot coals for 15 minutes on each side or to desired degree of doneness.

Yield: 8 servings

Party Steak Diane

1 (5-pound) sirloin steak,
    2 inches thick
1 teaspoon freshly ground
    pepper
1/2 cup (1 stick) butter
12 ounces fresh mushrooms,
    sliced
11/2 cups sliced green onions
2 teaspoons dry mustard
1/4 cup chopped fresh parsley
1 tablespoon lemon juice
1 tablespoon Worcestershire
    sauce
1 teaspoon salt

Let steak stand, covered, at room temperature for 1 hour. Trim excess fat; score edges at 1-inch intervals. Rub pepper into both sides. Melt butter in a skillet on grill over hot coals. Add mushrooms, green onions and dry mustard and sauté for 10 minutes or until onions are tender. Stir in parsley, lemon juice, Worcestershire sauce and salt; remove from heat. Rub hot grill with fat trimmings to prevent sticking. Grill steak 6 inches above hot coals for 15 minutes. Brush lightly with vegetable mixture. Grill for 5 minutes; turn. Grill for 20 minutes; brush lightly with vegetable mixture.

Yield: 8 servings

Quick & Easy Grilling

Onion-Buttered Sirloin

1 (4-pound) sirloin, 1¹/2 inches
    thick
¹/2 cup (1 stick) butter
¹/4 cup chopped fresh parsley
¹/4 cup minced onion
2 teaspoons Worcestershire
    sauce
¹/2 teaspoon dry mustard
¹/2 teaspoon pepper

Score edges of sirloin at 1-inch intervals. Combine butter, parsley, minced onion, Worcestershire sauce, dry mustard and pepper in saucepan. Heat until butter is melted, stirring constantly. Brush sauce on sirloin in shallow dish. Grill over hot coals for 5 minutes; turn. Baste with butter mixture. Grill for 2 minutes longer or to desired degree of doneness. Drizzle remaining sauce over individual servings.

Yield: 6 servings

Grilled Peppered Steak

2 cups veal stock
¹/4 cup pure maple syrup
1 cup apple cider
¹/4 cup balsamic vinegar
Salt and freshly cracked pepper
1 small red onion, minced
¹/2 green bell pepper, minced
4 apples, peeled, finely chopped
¹/4 cup (¹/2 stick) butter
¹/4 cup roasted chopped pecans
¹/4 cup pure maple syrup
3 tablespoons cider vinegar
2 tablespoons chopped
    fresh sage
4 (12-ounce) New York sirloin
    steaks

Combine veal stock, ¹/4 cup maple syrup and apple cider in saucepan; mix well. Simmer for 30 to 40 minutes or until reduced by ²/3. Stir in balsamic vinegar. Simmer for 10 minutes longer. Season with salt and pepper; set aside. Sauté onion, bell pepper and apples in butter in skillet for 3 to 4 minutes. Add pecans, ¹/4 cup maple syrup, cider vinegar, sage, salt and pepper. Sauté for 2 minutes longer. Adjust seasonings; set apple pecan relish aside. Rub steaks with pepper. Grill over medium-high heat for 4 to 5 minutes on each side. Arrange on serving plates. Spoon glaze over steaks. Serve with apple pecan relish.

Yield: 4 servings

Quick & Easy Grilling

Barbecued Strip Steak

8 (8-ounce) sirloin strip steaks
2 cups beef broth
1 cup vegetable oil
1/2 (4-ounce) bottle Heinz 57
　　Steak Sauce
1/2 (4-ounce) bottle A.1. Steak
　　Sauce
1 tablespoon Worcestershire
　　sauce
1 teaspoon onion powder
1 teaspoon salt
1/2 teaspoon freshly ground
　　pepper
1/2 teaspoon garlic powder

Place steaks in shallow dish. Combine the broth, oil, Heinz 57 Steak Sauce, A.1. Steak Sauce, Worcestershire sauce, onion powder, salt, pepper and garlic powder in bowl; mix well. Pour over steaks. Marinate, covered, in refrigerator for 3 to 4 hours, turning steaks every hour. Grill over hot coals until done to taste, basting frequently with marinade.

Yield: 8 servings

Carne Asada

4 (3/4-inch) beef rib-eye steaks
2 tablespoons fresh lime juice
8 (6-inch) flour tortillas
1/4 cup shredded Colby cheese
1/4 cup shredded Monterey Jack
　　cheese
1 cup salsa

Place steaks in shallow dish. Sprinkle with 1 tablespoon of the lime juice; turn steaks. Sprinkle with remaining lime juice. Grill steaks over medium-hot coals for 7 to 9 minutes or until a meat thermometer registers 140 degrees for rare or 160 degrees for medium, turning once. Wrap tortillas in heavy-duty foil. Place on outer edge of grill rack. Heat for 5 minutes, turning once. Cut steaks in half and arrange on serving platter; top each serving with Colby cheese and Monterey Jack cheese. Serve with warm tortillas and salsa.

Yield: 8 servings

Quick & Easy Grilling

Honey-Grilled Steaks and Onion

1/3 cup coarsely ground or
    regular Dijon mustard
1 1/2 tablespoons honey
1 tablespoon chopped fresh
    parsley
1 tablespoon cider vinegar
1 tablespoon water
1/4 teaspoon hot pepper sauce
1/8 teaspoon coarsely ground
    pepper
2 (1-inch) boneless beef top loin
    steaks, trimmed
1 large onion, cut into 1/2-inch
    slices

Combine Dijon mustard, honey, parsley, vinegar, water, hot pepper sauce and pepper in a bowl; mix well. Arrange steaks and onion slices on grill rack; brush both sides liberally with glaze. Grill over medium-hot coals for 9 to 12 minutes or until a meat thermometer registers 140 degrees for rare or 160 degrees for medium, turning and basting with glaze once. Cut steaks in half to serve.

Yield: 4 servings

Sesame Flank Steak

1/4 cup sesame seeds
1/4 cup sliced green onions
3 tablespoons soy sauce
2 tablespoons sesame oil
1 tablespoon vinegar
1 tablespoon brown sugar
1 tablespoon minced fresh
    gingerroot
1 tablespoon minced garlic
1 teaspoon dry mustard
1 teaspoon Worcestershire sauce
1 (1 1/2-pound) flank steak

Toast sesame seeds in skillet until golden brown. Combine sesame seeds, green onions, soy sauce, sesame oil, vinegar, brown sugar, gingerroot, garlic, dry mustard and Worcestershire sauce in bowl; mix well. Pour over steak in sealable plastic bag. Marinate in refrigerator for 8 to 10 hours, turning occasionally. Grill steak over hot coals for 6 to 7 minutes per side or to desired degree of doneness. Cut cross grain into thin slices to serve.

Yield: 4 servings

Quick & Easy Grilling

Flank Steak Nova Scotia

1 cup ketchup
1/2 cup water
1 tablespoon paprika
1 tablespoon sugar
1 garlic clove, minced
1 medium onion, finely chopped
1/3 cup vinegar
1 tablespoon Worcestershire
    sauce
1/4 cup (1/2 stick) butter
1 (1-pound) flank steak

Mix ketchup, water, paprika, sugar, garlic and onion in saucepan. Bring to a boil; reduce heat. Simmer for 10 minutes. Remove from heat and stir in next 3 ingredients. Cool to room temperature. Place steak in shallow dish and pour sauce over steak, coating completely. Marinate, covered, in refrigerator for 8 to 24 hours. Drain, reserving marinade. Prick steak with a fork on all sides. Grill steak over hot coals to desired degree of doneness. Cut steak crosswise into 1/2-inch to 1-inch slices to serve. Heat reserved marinade and serve as sauce.

Yield: 4 servings

Sirloin Mushroom Kabobs

2 tablespoons vegetable oil
1 medium onion, diced
1 (8-ounce) can tomatoes
1 garlic clove, minced
2 (4-ounce) cans chopped
    green chiles
1 (6-ounce) can tomato paste
1/2 cup water
1/3 cup orange juice
1 tablespoon brown sugar
1/4 teaspoon crushed red pepper
11/2 pounds sirloin steak, cubed
Sliced mushrooms, onions and
    green bell peppers

Heat oil in heavy skillet over high heat. Add onion and sauté until tender-crisp. Drain tomatoes. Add garlic, green chiles, tomatoes, tomato paste, water, orange juice, brown sugar and red pepper; mix well. Reduce heat and simmer for 10 minutes. Reserve about 1/2 cup of the tomato mixture; pour remaining mixture over sirloin in shallow dish. Marinate, covered, in refrigerator for 1 hour. Thread beef, mushrooms, onions and bell peppers alternately onto skewers until all ingredients are used. Grill over hot coals to desired degree of doneness, turning once. Serve with reserved sauce.

Yield: 6 servings

Quick & Easy Grilling

Shish Kabobs over the Coals

1/2 cup ketchup
1/4 cup water
2 tablespoons sugar
2 tablespoons each steak sauce,
    vinegar and Worcestershire
    sauce
2 tablespoons shortening
1 teaspoon salt
1 1/2 pounds steak, cut into cubes
8 large onion wedges
8 large green bell pepper pieces
8 cherry tomatoes
8 mushrooms
8 pineapple chunks

Combine ketchup, water, sugar, steak sauce, vinegar, Worcestershire sauce, shortening and salt in saucepan; mix well. Bring to a boil. Place steak cubes in bowl. Pour sauce over steak. Marinate, covered, in refrigerator for several hours to overnight. Drain, reserving sauce. Thread steak onto skewers, alternating with onion wedges, bell pepper, tomatoes, mushrooms and pineapple. Grill over hot coals to desired degree of doneness, basting with reserved sauce.

Yield: 4 servings

Barbecued Beef Kabobs

1 pound ground round
1/2 teaspoon meat tenderizer
1/2 cup bread crumbs
1/2 cup water
1 medium onion, grated
1 teaspoon garlic powder
1/4 teaspoon turmeric
1 egg, beaten
1/4 teaspoon pepper
1 teaspoon coriander
1 teaspoon cumin
Salt to taste
1/2 cup vegetable oil

Sprinkle ground round with tenderizer. Let stand, covered, for 30 minutes. Combine bread crumbs, water, onion, garlic powder, turmeric, egg, pepper, coriander, cumin and salt in a bowl; mix well. Combine with ground round and mix well. Shape into rolls. Thread lengthwise onto skewers. Brush with oil. Grill for 5 to 7 minutes on each side brushing with oil after turning.

Yield: 2 servings

Quick & Easy Grilling

Steak Fajitas

1 cup water
1/4 cup pineapple juice
1/4 cup orange juice
1/4 cup lemon juice
1/4 cup soy sauce
3 tablespoons clarified butter
3 dried chilies arboles,
    crumbled
2 tablespoons white wine
    vinegar
1 garlic clove, chopped
1 tablespoon pepper
1 teaspoon dried orange peel
1 teaspoon dried lemon peel
2 1/4 pounds round or skirt steak
Flour tortillas

Combine water, pineapple juice, orange juice, lemon juice, soy sauce, butter, chilies arboles, vinegar, garlic, pepper, orange peel and lemon peel in bowl; mix well. Pour over steak in glass dish. Marinate, covered, in refrigerator for up to 2 hours. Drain, reserving marinade. Grill steak over hot coals until done to taste, basting frequently with marinade. Slice thinly crosswise. Serve in tortillas with Pico de Gallo, guacamole and sour cream.

Yield: 4 to 6 servings

Barbecued Short Ribs

3 pounds beef short ribs
1/2 cup vinegar
1 envelope onion soup mix
1/4 cup sugar
2 tablespoons prepared brown
    mustard
1 1/2 cups ketchup
1/2 cup vegetable oil
1/2 cup vinegar
Hot pepper sauce to taste

Place ribs in Dutch oven. Add 1/2 cup vinegar and enough water to cover. Bring to a boil. Simmer, covered, for 45 minutes. Combine soup mix, sugar and prepared brown mustard in saucepan; mix well. Stir in ketchup, oil, 1/2 cup vinegar and hot pepper sauce. Bring mixture to a boil. Simmer for 20 minutes, stirring occasionally. Place ribs on grill over hot coals. Brown on all sides. Grill for 25 minutes, turning and basting with sauce occasionally.

Yield: 6 servings

Quick & Easy Grilling

Torpedo Burger

2 pounds lean ground beef

1 (8-ounce) can crushed
    pineapple, drained

1/3 cup chopped green onions

3 tablespoons soy sauce

1 teaspoon garlic powder

1 French baguette

3 tablespoons butter, melted

Salt to taste

1 green bell pepper, sliced into
    rings

1 tomato, sliced

Combine ground beef, pineapple, green onions, soy sauce and garlic powder in a bowl; mix well. Shape into a loaf resembling a French baguette in size. Place ground beef loaf on grill over medium coals and close cover. Grill for 20 minutes or until cooked through, turning once. Slice bread into halves lengthwise. Brush cut sides with butter. Place buttered sides down on warming rack of grill. Heat until golden. Place ground beef loaf on bottom half of bread. Season with salt. Layer bell pepper, tomato slices and top of bread over loaf. Cut into serving portions.

Yield: 4 to 6 servings

Spicy Burgers

1/3 cup crumbled blue cheese

4 scallions with tops, minced

1 red bell pepper, chopped

1 small yellow onion, minced

2 large garlic cloves, crushed

2 tablespoons soy sauce

1 tablespoon brown sugar

1 tablespoon Worcestershire
    sauce

1 tablespoon prepared
    horseradish

1 teaspoon pepper

2 pounds lean ground beef

Combine blue cheese, scallions, bell pepper, onion, garlic, soy sauce, brown sugar, Worcestershire sauce, horseradish and pepper in bowl and mix well. Add ground beef, stirring until mixed. Chill, covered, for 1 hour or longer. Shape into 8 patties. Grill over hot coals until cooked through.

Yield: 8 servings

Quick & Easy Grilling

Hamburgers Polynesian

1 pound ground beef
4 pineapple rings
1/2 cup ketchup
1/2 cup packed brown sugar
1/4 cup prepared mustard

Shape ground beef into 8 patties. Place 1 pineapple ring on half the patties; top with remaining patties, pressing edges to enclose pineapple. Combine ketchup, brown sugar and prepared mustard in saucepan. Heat to serving temperature, stirring to mix well. Grill patties over hot coals until cooked through. Serve with sauce.

Yield: 4 servings

Hamburgers on the Grill

2 pounds ground beef
1 egg, beaten
1 cup (4 ounces) shredded
    Cheddar cheese
1 cup chopped onion
1/2 cup ketchup
1 tablespoon Worcestershire
    sauce
1 teaspoon salt
1 teaspoon pepper
1/4 teaspoon oregano
8 hamburger buns

Combine ground beef, egg, cheese, onion, ketchup, Worcestershire sauce, salt, pepper and oregano in bowl; mix well. Shape into 8 patties. Grill over hot coals until done to taste. Serve on buns.

Yield: 8 servings

Quick & Easy Grilling

Charcoaled Meat Loaf

2 pounds ground beef
1 egg, beaten
1 onion, chopped
1/2 cup cracker crumbs
1/4 cup ketchup
2 tablespoons light brown sugar
1 teaspoon prepared mustard
1/4 cup ketchup
3 tablespoons brown sugar
1 teaspoon dry mustard
1/4 teaspoon nutmeg

Combine ground beef, egg, onion, cracker crumbs, 1/4 cup ketchup, 2 tablespoons brown sugar and prepared mustard in large bowl; mix well. Shape into loaf; place in lightly greased 10-inch baking pan. Grill over hot coals for 15 minutes. Place double thickness of foil on grill. Remove loaf to foil. Combine 1/4 cup ketchup, 3 tablespoons brown sugar, dry mustard and nutmeg in small bowl; mix well. Grill loaf for 10 minutes longer or until cooked through, basting with ketchup mixture.

Yield: 4 to 6 servings

Poor Man's Filets Mignons

1 1/2 pounds ground beef
1 small onion, chopped
1 egg, beaten
1/2 cup cracker crumbs
1 teaspoon Worcestershire sauce
Salt and pepper to taste
6 to 8 bacon slices

Combine ground beef, onion, egg, cracker crumbs, Worcestershire sauce, salt and pepper in bowl; mix well. Shape into 6 to 8 patties. Wrap 1 bacon slice around outer edge of each patty; secure with wooden pick. Grill until done to taste. Serve with buns if desired.

Yield: 6 to 8 servings

Quick & Easy Grilling

Meal-in-a-Bundle

2 pounds beef chuck, cubed
6 medium potatoes, chopped
6 carrots, sliced 1/4 inch thick
6 tablespoons chopped onion
1/2 cup chopped parsley
2 (10-ounce) cans golden
    mushroom soup
Tabasco sauce to taste
Salt and pepper to taste
3/4 cup water

Prepare six 18×18-inch pieces of foil. Layer 1/6 of the beef, potatoes, carrots, onion and parsley on each piece of foil. Spread with soup. Add Tabasco sauce, salt and pepper. Pour 2 tablespoons water over each serving. Fold foil over to enclose and seal edges tightly. Refrigerate until ready to cook. Grill 2 inches from medium coals for 1 hour. Serve from foil packet.

Yield: 6 servings

Grilled Meal-in-One

2 teaspoons margarine
2 1/2 cups sliced peeled potatoes
1/2 pound lean ground beef
Salt and pepper to taste
2 green onions, chopped
1/4 cup beef broth

Grease a 9-inch aluminum pie plate with margarine. Layer potatoes and ground beef in pie plate. Sprinkle with salt and pepper. Arrange chopped green onions over top. Pour beef broth over layers. Cover with foil, sealing edge. Grill over hot coals for 20 minutes or to desired degree of doneness.

Yield: 3 servings

Quick & Easy Grilling

Grilled Chili Dogs

10 (6-inch) flour tortillas
10 hot dogs
1 (15-ounce) can chili with
    beans
1¹/₂ cups (6 ounces) shredded
    American cheese
Sour cream to taste

Place each tortilla on a sheet of heavy-duty foil. Place hot dog in center of each tortilla. Top each with 2 tablespoons chili and 2 tablespoons cheese. Roll each tortilla to enclose filling. Secure with wooden picks. Wrap tightly with foil. Grill 4 to 6 inches above hot coals for 10 to 15 minutes or until heated through. Serve with sour cream.

Yield: 10 servings

Frank Kabobs

5 hot dogs
1 (20-ounce) can pineapple
    chunks, drained
1 (16-ounce) can potatoes,
    drained
1 pint cherry tomatoes
¹/₂ cup teriyaki sauce

Cut hot dogs into quarters. Thread hot dogs, pineapple, potatoes and tomatoes alternately onto skewers until all ingredients are used. Dip each skewer in teriyaki sauce. Grill over hot coals until heated through, turning frequently.

Yield: 5 servings

Quick & Easy Grilling

Grilled Lamb Chops

1 cup soy sauce
3/4 cup beef broth
1/2 cup sugar
1/4 cup red wine vinegar
12 lamb chops

Combine soy sauce, beef broth, sugar and vinegar in bowl and mix well. Place lamb chops in shallow dish and pour sauce over them, coating completely. Marinate, covered, in refrigerator overnight, turning occasionally. Grill chops over hot coals to desired degree of doneness.

Yield: 6 servings

Grilled Lamb Chops with Herbs

1/4 cup olive oil
1 garlic clove, minced
1 sprig of rosemary
Chopped fresh parsley to taste
6 lamb chops
Salt and white pepper to taste

Heat olive oil in skillet. Add garlic and sauté until tender. Add rosemary and parsley just before garlic turns golden in color. Remove from heat and cool. Season lamb chops with salt and white pepper. Coat chops with 3/4 of the herb mixture. Grill chops for 3 minutes on each side or to desired degree of doneness. Remove chops from heat, top with remaining herb mixture and serve.

Yield: 2 servings

Quick & Easy Grilling

Indonesian Satay

1/2 cup soy sauce
1 teaspoon molasses
1/2 cup roasted peanuts, ground
1/3 cup peanut butter
1 teaspoon hot red pepper
    flakes
1 garlic clove, minced
Juice of 1 lemon
3 pounds lamb or chicken, cut
    into 1-inch cubes
1 cup tomato sauce
1/4 cup water
Juice of 1 lemon
1 teaspoon Tabasco sauce

Mix soy sauce and molasses in medium saucepan. Add peanuts, peanut butter, red pepper flakes, garlic and lemon juice; mix well. Bring to a boil, stirring constantly. Cool to room temperature. Place lamb in shallow dish. Pour half the peanut sauce over lamb, coating completely. Reserve remaining sauce. Let stand for 1 hour. Thread lamb onto small bamboo skewers. Grill over hot coals for about 3 minutes on each side. Combine reserved peanut sauce, tomato sauce, water, lemon juice and Tabasco sauce in saucepan. Bring to a boil, stirring until smooth. Remove from heat. Serve lamb with hot sauce for dipping.

Yield: 6 servings

Lamb Shish Kabobs

1 (4- to 5-pound) leg of lamb or
    boned lamb shoulder
1 cup wine vinegar or cider
    vinegar
1/2 cup olive oil
2 large onions, chopped
2 garlic cloves, crushed
1 tablespoon oregano
Salt and pepper to taste
12 small tomatoes
8 to 10 small white onions
2 green bell peppers
2 red bell peppers

Cut lamb into 1 1/2-inch cubes. Combine vinegar, olive oil, chopped onions, garlic, oregano, salt and pepper in large bowl; mix well. Add lamb and marinate, covered, in refrigerator overnight. Cut tomatoes, small onions and bell peppers into 1 1/2-inch pieces. Thread lamb and vegetables alternately onto skewers until all ingredients are used. Grill over hot coals for 15 to 20 minutes, turning to brown on all sides, basting frequently with marinade. Cook to desired degree of doneness.

Yield: 4 to 6 servings

Quick & Easy Grilling

Barbecuing Pork

Oriental Grilled Pork Chops

1/2 cup teriyaki sauce
1/4 cup minced green onions
  with tops
1/4 cup lemon juice
2 tablespoons peanut oil
4 garlic cloves, minced
2 teaspoons crushed red pepper
4 (3/4-inch-thick) pork chops,
  trimmed

Mix teriyaki sauce, green onions, lemon juice, peanut oil, garlic and red pepper in bowl. Pour over pork chops in dish. Chill, covered, for 4 hours or longer, turning occasionally. Drain, reserving marinade. Grill pork chops 6 to 8 inches from hot coals for 30 to 45 minutes, turning and basting frequently with marinade.

Yield: 6 servings

Stuffed Pork Chops

1 cup coarsely chopped red bell
  pepper
1/2 cup thinly sliced red onion,
  separated into rings
1/4 cup chopped fresh cilantro
  or parsley
1 (10-ounce) package frozen
  whole kernel corn, thawed,
  drained
2 tablespoons cider vinegar
2 tablespoons vegetable oil
1/2 teaspoon cumin
1/4 teaspoon salt
1/4 teaspoon coarsely ground
  pepper
6 (1-inch-thick) pork chops

Combine bell pepper, onion, cilantro, corn, vinegar, oil, cumin, salt and pepper in medium bowl and mix well to make the corn relish. Split each pork chop from an outer edge toward the bone, making a pocket. Place about 2 tablespoons corn relish in each pocket. Grill for 20 minutes or until cooked through, turning occasionally. Serve remaining corn relish over pork chops.

Yield: 6 servings

Quick & Easy Grilling

Honey Gingered Pork Tenderloin

2 (12-ounce) pork tenderloins
1/4 cup honey
1/4 cup soy sauce
1/4 cup oyster sauce
2 tablespoons dark brown sugar
4 teaspoons minced fresh
   gingerroot
1 tablespoon minced garlic
1 tablespoon ketchup
1/4 teaspoon red pepper
1/4 teaspoon cinnamon

Place tenderloins in 7×11-inch baking dish. Combine honey, soy sauce, oyster sauce, brown sugar, gingerroot, garlic, ketchup, red pepper and cinnamon in small bowl; mix well. Pour over tenderloins. Marinate, covered, in refrigerator for 8 hours, turning occasionally. Remove tenderloins from marinade, reserving marinade. Grill tenderloins over medium hot coals for 25 to 35 minutes or until meat thermometer inserted into thickest portion of tenderloin registers 160 degrees. Turn often, basting with reserved marinade. Slice tenderloins thinly. Arrange on serving platter.

Yield: 6 servings

Italian Pork Tenderloin

1 envelope Italian salad
   dressing mix
Meat tenderizer to taste
1 (3-pound) pork tenderloin
1/3 cup red wine vinegar
1/4 cup ketchup
1 tablespoon minced garlic
1/4 cup soy sauce
1 tablespoon Worcestershire
   sauce
1 teaspoon prepared mustard
1/2 teaspoon black pepper
1 teaspoon MSG

Prepare salad dressing mix according to package directions, reserving 1/4 cup dressing. Sprinkle tenderizer over tenderloin. Combine vinegar, ketchup, garlic, soy sauce, Worcestershire sauce, prepared mustard, pepper, MSG and reserved salad dressing in shallow dish; mix well. Add tenderloin. Marinate in refrigerator for 6 to 8 hours. Place on middle rack of grill over low heat. Grill for 30 minutes, turning every 5 minutes.

Yield: 6 servings

Quick & Easy Grilling

Oriental Pork Tenderloin

1/2 cup peanut oil
1/3 cup soy sauce
1/4 cup red wine vinegar
3 tablespoons lemon juice
2 tablespoons Worcestershire
   sauce
1 garlic clove, minced
1 tablespoon chopped fresh
   parsley
1 tablespoon dry mustard
1 1/2 teaspoons pepper
2 (3/4- to 1-pound) pork
   tenderloins

Combine peanut oil, soy sauce, vinegar, lemon juice, Worcestershire sauce, garlic, parsley, dry mustard and pepper in a heavy-duty sealable plastic bag. Add tenderloins, turning to coat. Seal the plastic bag. Chill in refrigerator for 4 hours, turning occasionally; drain. Grill tenderloins 6 inches above medium-hot coals for 12 to 14 minutes or until cooked through, turning once.

Yield: 6 servings

Southwestern Stuffed Pork Tenderloin

3 pounds pork tenderloin
1 tomato, chopped
2 or 3 jalapeño chiles, chopped
1 bunch fresh cilantro, chopped
Juice of 1 lime
Salt to taste

Butterfly tenderloin. Combine tomato, jalapeño chiles, cilantro, lime juice and salt in bowl. Stuff tenderloin with mixture. Roll up and secure with string. Grill over hot coals for 25 minutes.

Yield: 6 to 8 servings

Quick & Easy Grilling

Layered Pork Medallions and Slaw

2 to 4 medallions of pork
   tenderloin
1 tablespoon soy sauce
2 teaspoons kosher salt
1 teaspoon cornstarch
1 small head cabbage, shredded
2 red bell peppers, minced
1/2 cup Dijon mustard
2 tablespoons vegetable oil
2 tablespoons vinegar
Salt and pepper to taste
1/2 cup molasses
1/2 cup balsamic vinegar
1 tablespoon chili powder

Pound pork to 1/2-inch thickness and place in shallow glass dish. Combine soy sauce, kosher salt and cornstarch in small bowl and blend well. Pour over pork and turn until coated. Marinate, covered, in refrigerator for 1 to 2 hours. Drain, reserving marinade. Grill over hot coals for 15 minutes or until cooked through, turning and basting frequently with reserved marinade. Combine cabbage, bell peppers, Dijon mustard, oil, vinegar, salt and pepper in medium bowl and mix well. Chill, covered, until ready to serve. Blend remaining ingredients in a small bowl. Layer cabbage mixture and grilled pork in large serving dish and drizzle with molasses mixture.

Yield: 2 to 4 servings

Jamaican Pork Tenderloin

1 pound lean pork tenderloin
3 tablespoons fresh lime juice
1 tablespoon bottled chopped
   jalapeño chile
1 teaspoon bottled minced
   garlic
1 cup bottled minced gingerroot
1/4 teaspoon salt
1/4 teaspoon allspice

Trim fat from tenderloin. Combine lime juice, jalapeño chile, garlic, gingerroot, salt and allspice in heavy-duty sealable plastic bag. Add tenderloin, turning to coat. Seal plastic bag. Chill in refrigerator for 30 minutes, turning occasionally. Drain, reserving marinade. Place tenderloin on grill rack coated with nonstick cooking spray. Grill, covered, over medium coals for 27 minutes or until meat thermometer registers 160 degrees. Cut into 1/4-inch-thick slices.

Yield: 4 servings

Quick & Easy Grilling

Grilled Pork Sandwiches

1 pork tenderloin, cut into
    1-inch cubes
3/4 cup lemon juice
1/2 cup olive oil
7 garlic cloves, chopped
1 tablespoon freshly ground
    pepper
2 teaspoons oregano
6 pita bread halves
1/2 cup chopped red onion
1 cup plain yogurt

Combine tenderloin, lemon juice, olive oil, garlic, pepper and oregano in bowl. Marinate, covered, in refrigerator for 24 hours, stirring occasionally; drain. Thread pork cubes onto skewers. Grill over hot coals for 3 minutes on each side or until browned and cooked through. Heat pita bread over coals. Place pork cubes in pita bread. Top with onion and yogurt.

Yield: 6 servings

Pork Loin Roast à l'Orange

1 (6-ounce) can frozen orange
    juice concentrate
1/4 cup wine vinegar
2 tablespoons brown sugar
2 tablespoons honey
2 teaspoons prepared mustard
2 teaspoons soy sauce
1 (5-pound) pork loin roast
Garlic salt to taste

Combine orange juice concentrate, vinegar, brown sugar, honey, prepared mustard and soy sauce in saucepan; mix well. Cook over low heat until blended, stirring frequently. Sprinkle roast with garlic salt. Grill over hot coals, basting with orange juice mixture every 20 minutes. Grill until meat thermometer registers 170 degrees. Cool for 5 to 10 minutes before slicing.

Yield: 10 servings

Quick & Easy Grilling

Pork and Chicken Fajitas

1 cup strong brewed coffee
1 (8-ounce) can tomato sauce
1/4 cup Worcestershire sauce
1/4 cup vegetable oil
3 tablespoons lime juice
1 tablespoon sugar
1 tablespoon pepper
1 (1-pound) pork roast or steak,
   thinly sliced
4 (4-ounce) boneless skinless
   chicken breasts, thinly sliced
8 (6-inch) flour tortillas

Combine coffee, tomato sauce, Worcestershire sauce, oil, lime juice, sugar and pepper in mixing bowl and beat until smooth. Pour evenly into 2 shallow bowls. Add pork to coffee mixture in 1 of the bowls, chicken to coffee mixture in the other. Marinate, covered, in refrigerator for 8 to 10 hours, turning pork and chicken occasionally. Drain pork and chicken, reserving marinade. Grill over hot coals for 6 minutes or to desired degree of doneness, basting frequently with reserved marinade.

Yield: 8 servings

Oriental Pork Kabobs

2 pounds boneless pork loin,
   cubed
1/4 cup soy sauce
1/4 cup peanut butter
1 tablespoon light brown sugar
1 tablespoon curry powder
2 tablespoons lemon juice
Dash of garlic powder
1/2 cup soy sauce
2 tablespoons peanut butter
1 tablespoon light brown sugar
1/2 teaspoon cayenne pepper
4 cups hot cooked rice

Mix pork with 1/4 cup soy sauce, 1/4 cup peanut butter, 1 tablespoon brown sugar, curry powder, lemon juice and garlic powder in bowl. Marinate, covered, in refrigerator overnight. Thread pork onto skewers and place on grill rack. Grill 6 to 8 inches from medium-hot coals for 20 minutes, turning frequently. Combine 1/2 cup soy sauce, 2 tablespoons peanut butter, 1 tablespoon brown sugar, and cayenne pepper in small bowl. Place pork kabobs over rice. Pour sauce over kabobs and serve.

Yield: 6 servings

Quick & Easy Grilling

Indonesian Pork

4 medium onions, chopped
2 garlic cloves, minced
1/4 cup soy sauce
3 tablespoons lemon juice
2 tablespoons brown sugar
4 teaspoons crushed coriander
    seeds
1 teaspoon each salt and pepper
1 1/2 pounds boned pork
    shoulder, trimmed, cut into
    1-inch pieces

Combine onions, garlic, soy sauce, lemon juice, brown sugar, coriander seeds, salt and pepper in glass bowl. Add pork. Marinate in refrigerator for 2 hours. Let stand at room temperature for 30 minutes. Drain pork; thread onto 6 skewers. Grill until pork is cooked through.

Yield: 6 servings

Pork and Vegetable Shish Kabobs

1 (6-ounce) can frozen orange
    juice concentrate, thawed
1 1/2 (6-ounce) orange juice cans
    water
1/2 cup soy sauce
1/4 cup light brown sugar
2 tablespoons Worcestershire
    sauce
1 garlic clove, crushed
Salt and pepper to taste
5 pounds pork loin, cut into
    1 1/2-inch cubes
Cherry tomatoes
Onion wedges
Bell pepper wedges
Fresh mushrooms (optional)

Combine orange juice concentrate, water, soy sauce, brown sugar, Worcestershire sauce, garlic, salt and pepper in large bowl; mix well. Place pork cubes in airtight container. Pour marinade over pork cubes; refrigerate, covered, overnight, stirring once or twice. Thread pork cubes on skewers alternating with vegetables until all ingredients are used. Grill over medium-hot coals for 10 to 15 minutes or until done, turning often and basting with marinade.

Yield: 10 to 12 servings

Quick & Easy Grilling

Vietnamese Pork en Brochette

6 to 8 tablespoons fish sauce
3 tablespoons sugar
1 tablespoon salt
1 tablespoon pepper
2 teaspoons garlic powder
1 green onion, chopped
3 pounds pork tenderloin
1 onion
1 green bell pepper
13 wooden skewers
Hot cooked rice or Chinese
    noodles

Combine fish sauce, sugar, salt, pepper, garlic powder and green onion in bowl; mix well. Cut tenderloin into 1-inch cubes. Cut onion and green pepper into wedges. Marinate tenderloin, onion and bell pepper in prepared sauce for at least 2 hours. Soak wooden skewers in water for 30 minutes. Thread tenderloin cubes on skewers alternating with vegetables until all ingredients are used. Grill over medium coals for 5 minutes on 1 side; turn. Grill for 2 minutes longer. Serve with rice or Chinese noodles.

Yield: 13 servings

Barbecued Pork Steaks

1 (15-ounce) can tomato sauce
1 small onion, chopped
1/4 cup soy sauce
2 tablespoons brown sugar
2 teaspoons curry powder
1 garlic clove, crushed
4 to 6 pork steaks or chops

Combine tomato sauce, onion, soy sauce, brown sugar, curry powder and garlic in small saucepan over medium heat and mix well. Bring to a boil. Reduce heat and simmer for 5 minutes. Cool. Place pork steaks and curry marinade in large sealable plastic bag, turning to coat. Chill for 4 to 10 hours. Remove pork steaks from bag, reserving marinade. Grill pork steaks over medium heat for 20 to 30 minutes or until cooked through, being careful not to burn. Place marinade in small saucepan and bring to a boil. Boil for 5 minutes. Serve with pork steaks.

Yield: 6 to 8 servings

Quick & Easy Grilling

Pork Steak Bundles

12 slices bacon

4 (1/2- to 3/4-inch) boneless pork
    steaks

4 (1/2-inch) slices white onion

1 large green bell pepper, cut
    into quarters

4 (1-ounce) slices American
    cheese

Arrange 2 slices of bacon in the shape of cross on work surface. Place 1 slice diagonally through center of cross. Layer 1 pork steak, 1 onion slice and 1 bell pepper quarter over bacon. Crisscross bacon over center; secure with wooden pick. Repeat process with remaining bacon, pork steaks, onion and bell pepper. Grill over medium-hot coals for 20 to 30 minutes or until cooked through. Top each bundle with 1 slice of cheese 3 minutes before end of cooking time.

Yield: 4 servings

Grilled Cranberry-Glazed Pork Roast

1 (4-pound) boneless pork
    roast, trimmed

1 (10-ounce) can beef broth

3/4 cup whole cranberry sauce

1/2 cup ketchup

1/2 envelope onion soup mix

2 garlic cloves, minced

1 teaspoon dry mustard

1/2 teaspoon marjoram

1/2 teaspoon salt

1/4 teaspoon pepper

8 medium potatoes, peeled,
    quartered

4 large carrots, quartered

Brown roast on all sides over medium-hot coals for 30 minutes. Whisk broth, cranberry sauce, ketchup, soup mix, garlic, dry mustard, marjoram, salt and pepper in medium bowl. Place half the sauce in center of a large piece of heavy-duty foil. Place roast on top of sauce. Top with potatoes and carrots; add remaining sauce. Fold foil to enclose and seal edges. Place on another piece of foil on grill rack. Grill over medium-hot coals for 1 1/2 to 2 hours or to desired degree of doneness.

Yield: 8 servings

Dry-Rub Barbecue Pork

2 cups hickory wood chips
1 (8- to 10-pound) Boston
   butt roast
5 tablespoons lemon pepper
   seasoned salt
1 teaspoon Hungarian paprika
1 teaspoon ground black pepper
1 teaspoon red pepper
1 teaspoon cumin
1 teaspoon chili powder

Soak wood chips in water to cover in bowl for 30 minutes; drain. Prepare and heat smoker using wood chips. Pat pork with paper towels. Combine seasonings in small bowl. Rub mixture onto all sides of roast wearing a plastic or rubber glove to make process easier. Place pork on rack in smoker. Slow-smoke for 5 to 6 hours or until cooked through, turning every hour and never allowing fire to flame; smoker should be cool enough to touch quickly with palm of hand. Pork will develop dark, crusty exterior and a 1/2- to 1-inch reddish smoke ring will penetrate into pork; pork will remain moist. Chop into bite-size pieces, discarding bone.

Yield: 10 servings

Boston Butt Roast

1 (4- to 6-pound) Boston butt
   roast
1/2 (10-ounce) bottle Dale's
   steak seasoning
Salt and pepper to taste
1 onion, chopped
1/2 each green, red and yellow
   bell pepper, chopped
Meat tenderizer to taste
Cajun seasoning to taste
Bacon bits

Place roast on 2 large sheets of heavy-duty foil. Pour Dale's seasoning over top. Sprinkle with salt and pepper. Arrange onion and bell peppers over top. Sprinkle with meat tenderizer and Cajun seasoning. Sprinkle bacon bits over top. Fold foil to enclose and seal edges. Grill over hot coals for 4 to 5 hours or until roast is cooked through and vegetables are tender.

Yield: 10 servings

Quick & Easy Grilling

Smoked Ribs with Honey Mustard Sauce

2 cups hickory wood chips
5 pounds pork spareribs
1/2 cup honey
1/4 cup prepared mustard
1/2 teaspoon maple extract

Soak wood chips in water to cover in bowl for 30 minutes; drain. Heat charcoal in smoker for 15 to 20 minutes or until coals are white. Arrange wood chips on coals. Fill water pan in smoker with water. Place spareribs on smoker rack. Cover with smoker lid. Cook for 3 hours. Combine honey, mustard and maple extract in saucepan. Cook over medium heat until blended, stirring constantly. Baste ribs with sauce. Cook, covered, for 30 minutes. Turn over ribs and baste again with sauce. Cook, covered, for 30 minutes longer or until cooked through.

Yield: 4 to 6 servings

Fantastic Ribs

1/2 cup soy sauce
1/4 cup beef or chicken broth
2 tablespoons light brown sugar
    or honey
1 teaspoon ginger
1/4 teaspoon dry mustard
1 large garlic clove, crushed
1 side pork ribs
2 tablespoons apricot preserves
1 tablespoon mustard
1 tablespoon honey

Combine soy sauce, broth, brown sugar, ginger, dry mustard and garlic in bowl; mix well. Pour over ribs in shallow dish. Marinate, covered, in refrigerator for 4 hours to overnight. Drain, reserving marinade. Combine preserves, mustard and honey in bowl; mix well. Place ribs on grill over High, browning on both sides. Reduce heat to Low. Grill until tender, basting each side with glaze the last 10 minutes of cooking. Wrap in heavy-duty foil; let stand for 10 minutes. Serve with reserved marinade.

Yield: variable

Quick & Easy Grilling

Tex-Mex Ribs

3 pounds spareribs or short ribs
1 (5-ounce) can tomato paste
1 cup water
1/4 cup packed light brown
    sugar
2 tablespoons red wine vinegar
1 garlic clove, crushed
1 teaspoon oregano
1/4 teaspoon cayenne pepper
3 tablespoons vegetable oil

Cut spareribs into serving-size pieces; place in large saucepan. Cover with boiling water; boil for 30 to 45 minutes. Combine tomato paste, water, brown sugar, vinegar, garlic, oregano and cayenne pepper in small saucepan. Simmer, uncovered, for 10 minutes, stirring often. Stir in oil. Brush ribs with sauce. Grill on well-greased grill rack about 5 inches above medium-hot coals for 20 minutes, turning and basting frequently.

Yield: 4 to 6 servings

Hawaiian Ham Steaks

1/4 cup prepared mustard
1/2 cup packed light brown
    sugar
2 tablespoons pineapple juice
1/8 teaspoon ground cloves
6 (1/2-inch-thick) ham steaks
1 (20-ounce) can pineapple
    slices

Mix prepared mustard, brown sugar, pineapple juice and cloves in bowl. Place ham steaks on grill over hot coals. Baste with mustard mixture. Grill for 6 minutes. Turn ham over; baste with mustard mixture. Place 2 pineapple slices on each steak. Grill for 6 minutes longer.

Yield: 8 to 12 servings

Quick & Easy Grilling

Ham Steak with English Cumberland Sauce

1 (14-ounce) jar spiced apple
    rings
1 cup packed brown sugar
1 teaspoon dry mustard
1 (1¹/2-inch-thick) ham steak
English Cumberland Sauce
    (below)

Drain apples, reserving juice. Combine reserved juice, brown sugar and dry mustard in shallow dish and mix well. Add ham steak and marinate, covered, for 2 hours. Grill over hot coals for 20 minutes, turning once. Place ham steak on serving platter. Arrange apple rings around ham steak. Serve with English Cumberland Sauce. Garnish with julienned lemon and orange peel.

Yield: 4 servings

English Cumberland Sauce

1 cup red currant jelly
1 cup orange juice
¹/2 cup chopped onion
¹/2 cup lemon juice
¹/2 grape juice
2 tablespoons red wine vinegar
1 tablespoon dry mustard
¹/4 teaspoon ginger
Tabasco sauce to taste
1¹/2 tablespoons arrowroot

Combine jelly, orange juice, onion, lemon juice, grape juice, vinegar, dry mustard, ginger and Tabasco sauce in saucepan and mix well. Bring to boil over medium heat, stirring frequently. Strain mixture, discarding onion. Return juice mixture to saucepan. Stir in arrowroot. Cook over medium heat until thickened, stirring constantly.

Quick & Easy Grilling

Poultry On The Grill

Grilled Turkey Breast

1 pound turkey breast
1/3 cup corn oil
1/4 cup white wine vinegar
1/4 cup lemon juice
1 tablespoon minced onion
1/2 teaspoon rosemary
1/4 teaspoon garlic powder

Cut turkey into 1/2-inch pieces. Place in shallow pan. Marinate, covered, in mixture of corn oil, vinegar, lemon juice, onion, rosemary and garlic powder for 4 hours to overnight in refrigerator; drain. Place turkey on sheet of heavy-duty foil. Fold foil to enclose and seal edges. Grill 3 to 4 inches above hot coals for about 10 minutes, turning once.

Yield: 4 servings

Turkey with Ginger Salsa

1/4 cup vinegar
2 tablespoons pineapple juice
2 tablespoons soy sauce
1 tablespoon grated fresh
    gingerroot
1 garlic clove, minced
1 teaspoon red pepper
4 (4-ounce) turkey breast
    tenderloins
1 medium tomato, peeled,
    seeded, chopped
1 green onion, chopped
1/4 cup green bell pepper,
    chopped
1 tablespoon chopped fresh
    cilantro
4 (6-inch) flour tortillas

Combine vinegar, pineapple juice, soy sauce, gingerroot, garlic and red pepper in sealable plastic bag; mix well. Reserve 2 tablespoons marinade. Rinse turkey and pat dry. Place in bag with marinade, turning to coat. Marinate in refrigerator for 1 hour. Combine reserved marinade with tomato, green onion, bell pepper and cilantro in bowl; mix well. Chill, covered, in refrigerator until ready to serve. Drain turkey, reserving marinade. Grill turkey over medium coals for 12 to 15 minutes, turning once and basting frequently with reserved marinade. Cut turkey into strips. Heat tortillas in single layer on grill for 15 seconds. Serve turkey with chilled salsa and warm tortillas.

Yield: 4 servings

Quick & Easy Grilling

Grilled Turkey Tenderloin

1 pound turkey tenderloin
1/4 cup soy sauce
1/4 cup vegetable oil
1/4 cup orange juice
2 tablespoons lemon juice
2 tablespoons dried onion
1/3 teaspoon ginger
1/8 teaspoon pepper, or to taste
1/8 teaspoon garlic salt, or
   to taste

Rinse turkey and pat dry. Mix soy sauce, oil, orange juice, lemon juice, onion, ginger, pepper and garlic salt in shallow pan. Add turkey, turning to coat both sides. Marinate, covered, in refrigerator for several hours, turning occasionally. Grill turkey over hot coals for 6 to 8 minutes per side or until cooked through. Turkey steaks are done when there is no pink in the center; do not overcook.

Yield: 4 servings

Mesquite Smoked Turkey

2 cups mesquite wood chips
3 to 4 ribs celery, chopped
1 onion, chopped
1 bay leaf, crushed
1 (11- to 13-pound) turkey
1/2 cup (1 stick) melted butter
2 tablespoons Cajun seasoning
15 pounds charcoal briquets
4 quarts hot water

Soak wood chips in water to cover in bowl for 30 minutes; drain. Mix celery, onion and bay leaf in bowl. Rinse turkey and pat dry. Rub inside and outside generously with butter and Cajun seasoning. Stuff turkey with celery mixture. Arrange briquets in smoker. Arrange wet mesquite chips over briquets. Pour water into water pan. Place turkey on smoker grill. Smoke, covered, at 170 degrees for 10 to 12 hours, checking occasionally and adding additional water if necessary.

Yield: 12 servings

Quick & Easy Grilling

Grilled Whole Turkey with Lime

1 (12-pound) turkey
1/2 cup (1 stick) butter or
    margarine
Juice of 6 limes
2 tablespoons orange juice
2 tablespoons finely chopped
    fresh oregano, or 1 teaspoon
    dried oregano
Salt and freshly ground pepper
    to taste

Have butcher butterfly turkey. Cut off excess skin and fat. Rinse and pat dry. Insert meat thermometer in thickest part not touching bone. Melt butter in saucepan. Add lime juice, orange juice, oregano, salt and pepper and mix well. Place turkey skin side down on oiled grill about 6 inches above heat. Mop turkey with lime mixture. Grill for 1 1/2 to 2 hours or until meat thermometer reads 170 degrees, turning and basting with lime mixture every 15 minutes.

Yield: 6 servings

Spicy Turkey Fajitas

6 turkey breast fillets
1/2 teaspoon garlic powder
1/2 teaspoon cayenne pepper
1/2 teaspoon chili powder
1/2 teaspoon cumin
8 flour tortillas, warmed
2 tomatoes, chopped
1 white onion, chopped
1 cup (4 ounces) shredded
    Cheddar cheese
1 avocado, sliced
1 cup sour cream
1 cup picante sauce or salsa

Rinse turkey and pat dry. Combine garlic powder, cayenne pepper, chili powder and cumin in sealable plastic bag. Add turkey to bag. Shake to coat well. Shake off excess seasonings. Grill turkey until tender. Cut into lengthwise slices. Serve with warm tortillas, tomatoes, onion, cheese, avocado, sour cream and picante sauce.

Yield: 4 servings

Quick & Easy Grilling

Chicken Breasts Supreme

3 tablespoons soy sauce
3 tablespoons teriyaki sauce
2 tablespoons honey
1 tablespoon lemon juice
2 garlic cloves, sliced
Dash of ginger
Dash of pepper
4 to 6 skinless chicken breasts
Hot cooked rice

Combine soy sauce, teriyaki sauce, honey, lemon juice, garlic, ginger and pepper in small bowl; mix well. Place chicken in shallow dish; pour marinade over chicken. Marinate, covered, in refrigerator for 2 hours, turning frequently. Drain, reserving marinade. Grill chicken on Medium-Low for 40 to 50 minutes or until tests done, turning frequently, basting with reserved marinade. Serve over hot cooked rice.

Yield: 4 to 6 servings

Grilled Curried Chicken

16 ounces bitter orange
  marmalade
1 cup finely ground salted
  peanuts
1 (6-ounce) jar Dijon mustard
1/2 cup olive oil
1/2 cup fresh orange juice
1/4 cup fresh tarragon leaves, or
  2 tablespoons dried tarragon
2 teaspoons curry powder
1 teaspoon salt
8 chicken breasts
1 cup shredded coconut
1 cup dried currants

Combine marmalade, peanuts, Dijon mustard, olive oil, orange juice, tarragon, curry powder and salt in shallow baking dish; mix well. Rinse chicken and pat dry. Add to marinade, coating well. Marinate, covered, in refrigerator for 4 to 6 hours, turning occasionally. Bake chicken in marinade at 350 degrees for 35 minutes. Drain, reserving marinade. Grill 4 inches from hot coals for 8 to 10 minutes on each side or until cooked through, brushing frequently with marinade. Arrange chicken on serving platter; sprinkle with coconut and currants.

Yield: 8 servings

Quick & Easy Grilling

Lemon Pepper Chicken

1 cup (2 sticks) melted butter
1 cup sweet-and-sour mix
1/4 cup lemon pepper seasoning
2 tablespoons garlic salt
1 pound chicken breasts

Combine butter, sweet-and-sour mix, lemon pepper seasoning and garlic salt in bowl. Add chicken. Marinate for 30 minutes. Drain, reserving marinade. Grill over hot coals until brown on 1 side. Dip in marinade. Grill until brown and tender.

Yield: 2 servings

Grilled Chicken Caesar Pizza

3 boneless skinless chicken
  breasts, trimmed
1 envelope Caesar salad
  dressing mix
5 tablespoons olive oil
3 tablespoons white wine
  vinegar
1 tablespoon grated Parmesan
  cheese
1 (14-ounce) Boboli pizza crust
1 tablespoon olive oil
8 ounces rope provel cheese
3 large leaves romaine, coarsely
  chopped
2 Roma tomatoes, chopped

Rinse chicken and pat dry. Pound 1/4 inch thick between sheets of plastic wrap. Place chicken in large sealable plastic bag. Reserve 1 tablespoon of dressing mix. Place remaining dressing mix in small jar with tight-fitting lid. Add 5 tablespoons olive oil and vinegar; cover and shake well. Reserve 2 tablespoons of dressing; pour remaining dressing over chicken; seal bag and turn to coat. Refrigerate for several hours, turning occasionally; drain. Grill for 4 to 5 minutes per side. Combine reserved dressing mix with Parmesan cheese in small bowl. Brush pizza crust with 1 tablespoon olive oil. Sprinkle with Parmesan mixture. Place on piece of heavy-duty foil. Grill over medium coals for 5 minutes. Cut chicken into thin slices. Arrange over prepared crust. Top with provel cheese. Grill for 4 to 5 minutes or until cheese melts. Drizzle reserved dressing over lettuce and tomatoes; toss to coat. Top pizza with lettuce mixture.

Yield: 6 servings

Quick & Easy Grilling

Grapefruit Chicken Breasts

4 (8-ounce) chicken breasts
1/2 cup vegetable oil
Juice of 2 lemons
Juice of 1 grapefruit
1/4 teaspoon thyme
1/4 teaspoon rosemary
1/4 teaspoon salt
1/4 teaspoon pepper

Place chicken in shallow dish. Combine oil, lemon juice, grapefruit juice, thyme, rosemary, salt and pepper in bowl; mix well. Pour over chicken. Refrigerate, covered, for 24 hours, turning occasionally. Grill over medium-hot coals until done, turning and basting with marinade. May garnish with citrus slices if desired.

Yield: 4 servings

Pechugas Bahia

6 boneless skinless chicken
    breasts
Salt and pepper to taste
1/4 cup olive oil
1 tablespoon minced garlic
3/4 cup unsweetened coconut
    milk
1/2 cup (1 stick) butter, softened
Juice of 1 lime
3/4 cup chopped seeded
    tomatoes
1 jalapeño chile, seeded, veined,
    finely chopped
6 large (1×5-inch) hearts of
    palm, sliced thinly on the
    diagonal
3/4 cup chopped fresh cilantro

Season chicken with salt and pepper. Mix olive oil and garlic in small bowl. Grill chicken until cooked through, basting with garlic-olive oil mixture; keep warm. Heat (do not boil) coconut milk in medium saucepan over low heat. Add butter gradually, whisking to incorporate. Remove from heat; add lime juice, chopped tomatoes, jalapeño chile and hearts of palm. Season with salt and adjust flavors to taste. Arrange each chicken breast on a plate; spoon on sauce. Sprinkle with cilantro.

Yield: 6 servings

Quick & Easy Grilling

Peppered Chicken Breasts with Rosemary and Garlic

2 tablespoons fresh lemon juice
2 tablespoons olive oil
1/2 teaspoon rosemary
1/8 to 1/4 teaspoon crushed hot red pepper
1/2 to 1 teaspoon coarsely cracked black pepper
4 garlic cloves, minced
4 boneless skinless chicken breasts

Combine lemon juice, olive oil, rosemary, red pepper, black pepper and garlic in large bowl; mix well. Rinse chicken and pat dry. Add chicken to marinade, turning to coat. Marinate, covered, in refrigerator for 1 hour, turning 1 or 2 times; drain. Grill chicken over medium-hot coals until cooked through.

Yield: 4 servings

Chicken with Asparagus

4 chicken breast fillets
1 1/2 pounds asparagus, trimmed, cut into 1 1/2-inch pieces
12 ounces fresh mushrooms, sliced
1 small onion, cut into halves, sliced
4 teaspoons water
4 to 8 sprigs of rosemary
Salt and pepper to taste

Rinse chicken and pat dry. Cut into chunks or strips. Cut 4 pieces of foil; spray with nonstick cooking spray. Place 1/4 of the chicken, asparagus, mushrooms and onion on each foil piece. Add 1 teaspoon water and 1 or 2 sprigs of rosemary to each packet; sprinkle with salt and pepper. Fold foil to enclose and seal edges. Grill for 10 to 15 minutes, turning once.

Yield: 4 servings

Quick & Easy Grilling

Jamaica Jerk War Eagles

2 tablespoons salt
2 tablespoons garlic powder
1 tablespoon sugar
1 tablespoon allspice
1 tablespoon thyme
1 1/2 teaspoons cayenne pepper
1 1/2 teaspoons black pepper
1 1/2 teaspoons sage
3/4 teaspoon nutmeg
3/4 teaspoon cinnamon
3/4 cup white vinegar
1/2 cup orange juice
1/4 cup lime juice
1/4 cup olive oil
1/4 cup soy sauce
1 Scotch bonnet chile, seeded,
    finely chopped
1 white onion, finely chopped
3 green onions, finely chopped
4 large chicken breasts

Combine salt, garlic powder, sugar, allspice, thyme, cayenne pepper, black pepper, sage, nutmeg and cinnamon in large bowl; mix well. Add vinegar, orange juice, lime juice, olive oil and soy sauce gradually, blending well with wire whisk. Stir in Scotch bonnet chile, white onion and green onions. Rinse chicken and pat dry. Add to marinade. Marinate, covered, in refrigerator for 1 hour or longer. Drain, reserving marinade. Grill chicken for 6 to 8 minutes on each side, basting with reserved marinade. Heat leftover marinade to serve with chicken. Chicken may be shredded like barbecue after grilling.

Yield: 4 servings

Grilled Chicken Pesto

6 tomatoes, chopped
2 tablespoons basil pesto
1 tablespoon fresh lemon juice
Salt to taste
3 cups cooked angel hair pasta
6 boneless chicken breasts,
    grilled

Sauté tomatoes in nonstick skillet until juices separate. Add pesto, lemon juice and salt; mix well. Place 1/2 cup hot angel hair pasta on each plate; top with chicken. Spoon tomato pesto sauce over chicken.

Yield: 6 servings

Quick & Easy Grilling

Raspberry Mustard Chicken

4 chicken cutlets

5 tablespoons Dijon mustard

3 tablespoons raspberry vinegar

1 tablespoon fresh rosemary,
    tarragon and/or thyme

1 garlic clove, minced

2 teaspoons coarse-grain
    mustard

2 tablespoons fresh rosemary,
    tarragon and/or thyme

2 tablespoons raspberry vinegar

3 tablespoons extra-virgin
    olive oil

3 tablespoons chicken stock

Salt and pepper to taste

4 romaine leaves

1/4 cup raspberries

Rinse chicken and pat dry. Pound cutlets to uniform thickness. Mix Dijon mustard, 3 tablespoons vinegar and 1 tablespoon herbs in large bowl. Add chicken, turning to coat. Marinate, covered, in refrigerator for 1 hour. Grill chicken for 2 to 4 minutes per side or until cooked through; do not overcook. Mix garlic, coarse-grain mustard, 2 tablespoons herbs and 2 tablespoons vinegar in bowl. Whisk in olive oil and stock. Season with salt and pepper. Arrange chicken on romaine leaves. Spoon sauce over chicken and top with raspberries.

Yield: 4 servings

Grilled Herbed Chicken

1/2 teaspoon basil

1/2 teaspoon thyme

1/2 teaspoon oregano

6 boneless skinless chicken
    breasts

1 tablespoon olive oil

Juice of 1 lemon

Combine basil, thyme and oregano in small bowl and mix well. Trim excess fat from chicken. Rinse and pat dry. Pound 1/4 inch thick between sheets of waxed paper. Brush chicken with olive oil. Sprinkle lemon juice and herb mixture over top. Coat grill rack with nonstick cooking spray. Grill chicken 6 inches above medium coals for 10 minutes or until chicken is tender, turning once.

Yield: 6 servings

Quick & Easy Grilling

Mustard Pepper Chicken with Herb Sauce

5 shallots, coarsely chopped

5 large mushrooms, cut into
    quarters

1 teaspoon pepper

1 tablespoon unsalted butter

1 cup chicken stock

5 sprigs of fresh rosemary, or
    $1/2$ teaspoon dried rosemary

5 sprigs of fresh thyme, or
    $1^1/2$ teaspoons dried thyme

2 cups chicken stock

8 boneless skinless chicken
    breasts

5 teaspoons pepper

$1/4$ cup Dijon mustard

1 tablespoon whole yellow
    mustard seeds

$1/2$ teaspoon minced fresh
    thyme, or $1/4$ teaspoon
    dried thyme

1 tablespoon unsalted butter

Hot mashed potatoes

Steamed green beans

Sauté shallots and mushrooms with 1 teaspoon pepper in 1 tablespoon butter in large heavy skillet over medium heat for 8 minutes or until brown. Stir in 1 cup stock. Bring to a boil. Add rosemary and 5 sprigs of thyme. Simmer for 5 minutes. Add 2 cups stock. Cook for about 20 minutes or until liquid is reduced to $3/4$ cup, stirring occasionally. Strain into saucepan, reserving vegetables and herbs. Keep vegetables and herbs warm in 250-degree oven. Rinse chicken and pat dry. Sprinkle with 5 teaspoons pepper. Grill chicken over hot coals for 5 minutes on each side or until cooked through. Remove to broiler pan. Brush chicken with Dijon mustard; sprinkle with mustard seeds. Broil for 2 minutes or until brown. Remove to hot serving platter; keep warm in 250-degree oven. Bring herb sauce to a boil. Add $1/2$ teaspoon thyme and 1 tablespoon butter. Cook until butter is melted, stirring occasionally. Arrange chicken, vegetables and herbs on 4 serving plates. Spoon hot herb sauce over chicken. Serve with mashed potatoes and green beans. May make herb sauce 1 day ahead and chill, covered, in refrigerator.

Yield: 4 servings

Cranberry-Glazed Chicken Halves

4 small chickens, split
1/2 cup cranberry juice cocktail
1/2 cup chicken broth
1/4 cup vegetable oil
2 tablespoons red wine vinegar
1 tablespoon rosemary
1 teaspoon black peppercorns
1/2 teaspoon salt

Disjoint the chicken wings and discard the tips. Combine cranberry juice cocktail, chicken broth, oil, vinegar, rosemary, peppercorns and salt in bowl and mix well. Add chickens. Marinate, covered, in refrigerator for 1 hour, turning once. Drain, reserving the marinade. Place skin side up on grill 5 inches above coals. Grill for 15 minutes, brushing with reserved marinade. Turn chickens. Grill until tender.

Yield: 8 servings

Aloha Chicken and Pineapple

1 (16-ounce) can pineapple
  chunks
6 to 8 boneless skinless chicken
  breasts
1/2 cup teriyaki sauce
1 cup packed dark brown sugar

Soak wooden skewers in water. Drain pineapple, reserving juice. Place chicken, reserved juice, teriyaki sauce and brown sugar in 1-gallon sealable plastic bag. Shake gently to coat. Chill for 4 hours to overnight. Remove chicken from bag with tongs; place on hot grill. Grill for 10 minutes or until cooked through, turning after 5 minutes. Thread pineapple chunks onto skewers; place on outer edges of grill. Grill for 5 minutes on each side.

Yield: 6 to 8 servings

Quick & Easy Grilling

Bacon-Wrapped Chicken and Mushroom Kabobs

2 large chickens, boned
10 large mushrooms, cut in half
1/4 cup soy sauce
1/4 cup cider vinegar
2 tablespoons honey
2 tablespoons vegetable oil
2 small green onions, minced
1 (8-ounce) can sliced
    pineapple, drained
8 ounces sliced bacon

Cut chicken into 1¹/₂-inch pieces. Combine chicken, mushrooms, soy sauce, vinegar, honey, oil and green onions in large bowl. Cut each pineapple slice into 3 pieces. Cut each bacon slice into pieces; wrap bacon pieces around chicken chunk and mushroom half. Thread onto skewers, alternating with pineapple pieces, leaving space between each so bacon can cook completely. Grill over medium-hot coals for about 20 minutes, turning once, basting with sauce.

Yield: 4 servings

Surf and Turf Kabobs

4 cups cubed chicken
4 cups cubed flank or tenderloin
    steak
2 cups cubed orange roughy
2 cups mushrooms
2 cups green bell pepper pieces
3 cups cherry tomatoes
2 cups eggplant pieces
2 cups onion wedges
2 cups fresh pineapple chunks

Thread chicken, steak, orange roughy, mushrooms, bell peppers, tomatoes, eggplant, onion and pineapple alternately onto skewers until all ingredients are used. Grill over hot coals to desired degree of doneness.

Yield: variable

Quick & Easy Grilling

Chicken Tender Kabobs

1 pound chicken breast fillets
1 onion, cut into quarters
1 each green and red bell
   pepper, cut into squares
8 ounces mushroom caps
1 small onion, chopped
1 garlic clove, crushed
2 tablespoons lemon juice
1 tablespoon soy sauce
1 teaspoon olive oil
1/2 cup low-sodium soy sauce
1 teaspoon lemon juice
1/2 teaspoon chili powder
1/4 teaspoon crushed garlic
1/4 teaspoon finely chopped
   fresh gingerroot

Cut chicken into 1-inch cubes. Thread onto skewers alternating with onion quarters, bell peppers and mushrooms. Place in shallow dish. Add mixture of chopped onion, garlic, lemon juice, 1 tablespoon soy sauce and olive oil. Marinate, covered, in refrigerator for 1 to 3 hours; drain. Mix 1/2 cup soy sauce, lemon juice, chili powder, garlic and gingerroot in bowl. Grill chicken over hot coals until tender, basting frequently with sauce. Serve with remaining sauce.

Yield: 4 servings

Chicken and Apple Cider Sauce

10 chicken pieces
1 cup apple cider vinegar
1/2 cup vegetable oil
1 1/2 teaspoons salt
3/4 teaspoon poultry seasoning
1/2 teaspoon pepper
1 egg, lightly beaten

Rinse chicken and pat dry. Combine chicken with water to cover in saucepan. Cook until tender. Drain, reserving broth for another use. Combine vinegar, oil, salt, poultry seasoning, pepper and egg in 1-quart jar with tight-fitting lid. Shake, covered, until mixed. Pour marinade over the chicken in large nonreactive dish. Chill, covered, for 4 to 6 hours. Drain, reserving marinade. Grill until light brown, basting with marinade.

Yield: 10 servings

Quick & Easy Grilling

Barbecued Chicken

1/2 cup vegetable oil
1/2 cup tomato sauce
1/2 cup red wine vinegar
2 large garlic cloves, finely
　chopped
1 tablespoon Worcestershire
　sauce
1 teaspoon salt
1 teaspoon sugar
1 teaspoon dry mustard
2 or 3 drops of liquid smoke
Dash of pepper
2 chickens, cut up

Combine oil, tomato sauce, vinegar, garlic, Worcestershire sauce, salt, sugar, dry mustard, liquid smoke and pepper in jar with tight-fitting lid. Shake, covered, until well mixed. Refrigerate, covered, overnight. Place chicken in shallow dish. Pour sauce over chicken. Marinate, covered, in refrigerator for 4 to 5 hours, stirring occasionally. Drain, reserving marinade. Grill chicken over medium heat for 1 to 1 1/2 hours, turning and basting with reserved marinade.

Yield: 8 to 12 servings

Tarragon Dijon Chicken

1/4 cup olive oil
1/4 cup Dijon mustard
3 tablespoons lemon juice
3 tablespoons lime juice
2 garlic cloves, minced
1 teaspoon tarragon
1/2 teaspoon pepper
8 chicken thighs, skinned
Lime slices

Combine olive oil, Dijon mustard, lemon juice, lime juice, garlic, tarragon and pepper in shallow dish. Add chicken. Chill, covered, for 30 minutes, turning occasionally. Remove chicken from marinade. Grill chicken, covered with grill lid, over medium-hot coals for 8 to 10 minutes on each side or until cooked through. Top with lime slices.

Yield: 4 servings

Quick & Easy Grilling

24-Hour Marinated Chicken

1 cup corn oil
1/2 cup cider vinegar
1/4 cup Worcestershire sauce
3 tablespoons lime juice
1 tablespoon each paprika,
   garlic salt, salt and sugar
1 teaspoon Tabasco sauce
1 teaspoon garlic powder
1/2 teaspoon pepper
2 chickens, cut up

Combine corn oil, vinegar, Worcestershire sauce, lime juice, paprika, garlic salt, salt, sugar, Tabasco sauce, garlic powder and pepper in blender and process until smooth. Pour over chicken in large bowl. Marinate in refrigerator for 24 hours. Grill chicken over medium coals for 45 to 60 minutes, turning and basting constantly.

Yield: 8 servings

Lemon-Lime Sparkling Chicken

2 cups 7-Up
2 cups corn oil
1 cup soy sauce
1 tablespoon horseradish
1 tablespoon garlic salt
2 or 3 chickens, cut up

Combine 7-Up, corn oil, soy sauce, horseradish and garlic salt in large bowl. Add chicken. Marinate, covered, in refrigerator for 24 hours. Grill over hot coals until tender, basting frequently with marinade.

Yield: 6 servings

Lime and Hot Pepper Chicken

1/3 cup vegetable oil
3 tablespoons soy sauce
1 tablespoon lime juice
1 teaspoon grated lime zest
1/2 teaspoon hot pepper sauce
1 chicken, cut up

Whisk first 5 ingredients in bowl. Reserve 3 tablespoons. Combine chicken with marinade in sealable plastic bag. Marinate in refrigerator for 30 minutes or longer. Grill chicken over hot coals until done, turning and basting frequently with reserved marinade.

Yield: 6 servings

Quick & Easy Grilling

From The Sea

Fish and Vegetable Foil Packets

Lettuce leaves

4 (1-pound) bass, perch or
    redfish

Margarine

1 tomato, sliced

1 onion, sliced

1 green bell pepper, sliced

Paprika to taste

Freshly ground pepper to taste

Garlic salt to taste

Lemon juice to taste

Worcestershire sauce to taste

Line baking pan with foil then with lettuce leaves to prevent fish from sticking. Cover fish with margarine. Arrange tomato, onion and bell pepper slices under, inside and on top of fish. Sprinkle with paprika, pepper and garlic salt. Add lemon juice and Worcestershire sauce. Seal with foil. Grill over hot coals until foil steams.

Yield: 8 servings

Blackened Redfish

1 tablespoon paprika

2 1/2 teaspoons salt

1 teaspoon onion powder

1 teaspoon garlic powder

1 teaspoon red pepper

3/4 teaspoon white pepper

3/4 teaspoon black pepper

1/2 teaspoon thyme

1/2 teaspoon oregano

3 pounds redfish fillets

1/4 cup (1/2 stick) butter, melted

Mix paprika, salt, onion powder, garlic powder, red pepper, white pepper, black pepper, thyme and oregano in small shallow bowl. Dip fillets into melted butter. Coat with spice mixture. Preheat cast-iron skillet over grill until very hot. Place fillets in skillet. Cook for 2 minutes; turn redfish over. Grill for 1 minute longer. This is smoky when prepared; cook outside or in well-ventilated area.

Yield: 8 servings

Quick & Easy Grilling

Catfish Fillets

1/2 cup (1 stick) butter, melted
4 catfish fillets
1 cup chopped onion
1 teaspoon paprika

Spread melted butter on baking sheet. Arrange fillets in butter. Top with onion and sprinkle with paprika. Place baking sheet on grill rack. Grill fillets for 5 minutes after pan is hot. Turn fillets and grill for 5 minutes longer.

Yield: 4 servings

Grilled Fish with Banana Sauce

2 pounds firm white fish fillets
Flour
Vegetable oil for panfrying
1 tablespoon butter or margarine
1 tablespoon flour
1 cup pineapple juice
1 teaspoon almond extract
2 firm Bermuda bananas, sliced
Juice of 1/2 lemon or lime
1 tablespoon sugar
1 tablespoon curry powder
1/2 teaspoon salt
1/2 teaspoon freshly ground
  pepper
Hot cooked rice
Grilled tomatoes
Buttered green peas

Coat fillets with flour in bowl. Panfry in a small amount of oil in skillet over medium coals until tender; set aside. Melt 1 tablespoon butter in medium saucepan over medium coals. Add 1 tablespoon flour; mix well. Add pineapple juice and almond extract gradually, mixing with fork. Add bananas, lemon juice, sugar, curry powder, salt and pepper. Cook over low heat until slightly thickened. Serve over fish fillets. Serve with rice, grilled tomatoes and buttered green peas.

Yield: 4 servings

Quick & Easy Grilling

Grilled Mahimahi with Fruit

4 (6-ounce) mahimahi fillets
Salt and pepper to taste
1 whole pineapple, minced
1/2 cantaloupe, minced
1/2 honeydew melon, minced
1/4 cup honey
2 strawberries, halved
Chopped fresh mint

Season the mahimahi with salt and pepper. Grill 3 to 4 minutes on each side. Combine the pineapple, cantaloupe, honeydew and honey in a bowl and mix well. Divide the fruit mixture among 4 dinner plates. Top with grilled mahimahi. Garnish with half a strawberry and mint.

Yield: 4 servings

Mahimahi in Red Onion Butter

4 (8-ounce) mahimahi fillets
2 tablespoons extra-virgin
   olive oil
2 medium red onions,
   sliced 1/8 inch thick
Freshly ground white pepper
   to taste
3 tablespoons extra-virgin
   olive oil
1 sprig of thyme
1/2 cup chicken or vegetable
   broth
1/2 cup whipping cream
Salt and pepper to taste
1/4 cup (1/2 stick) unsalted butter

Drizzle mahimahi with 2 tablespoons olive oil in shallow dish. Top with 4 slices onion and white pepper. Cover and marinate for 2 to 3 hours in refrigerator. Sauté remaining onion slices in 3 tablespoons olive oil in skillet until tender-crisp and light golden brown. Stir in thyme leaves. Add broth, stirring to deglaze pan. Cook until broth is reduced by half. Stir in cream. Cook until sauce is slightly reduced. Season with salt and pepper. Whisk in butter gradually. Keep sauce warm. Remove mahimahi from marinade; season on both sides with salt. Grill over mesquite fire just until fish feels slightly springy to the touch. Spoon onion butter sauce onto 4 warm plates. Top with grilled mahimahi. Garnish with small sprigs of thyme.

Yield: 4 servings

Quick & Easy Grilling

Salmon Burgers

1 (1-pound) boneless skinless
    salmon fillet, finely chopped
2 tablespoons bread crumbs
1 tablespoon Dijon mustard
1 tablespoon minced onion
2 teaspoons lemon juice
1/2 teaspoon minced or pressed
    garlic
1/2 teaspoon salt, or to taste
1/2 teaspoon freshly ground
    pepper
4 hamburger buns
1 1/2 to 2 tablespoons
    mayonnaise or tartar sauce

Combine salmon, bread crumbs, Dijon mustard, onion, lemon juice, garlic, salt and pepper in a bowl and mix well. Shape into four 1/2×4-inch patties; patties will be fragile. Place on a plate. Chill until needed. Place patties 2 inches apart on grill rack. Grill over medium-hot coals for 2 minutes per side or just until cooked through, turning once. Serve on buns and spread with mayonnaise or tartar sauce.

Yield: 4 servings

Salmon with Basil Mustard Crust

3 tablespoons Dijon mustard
3 tablespoons fresh basil,
    minced
1/2 teaspoon olive oil
1 pound (1-inch) skinless
    salmon fillets

Mix the Dijon mustard, basil and olive oil in small bowl. Spread generously on both sides of salmon. Refrigerate until ready to cook. Spray grill rack with nonstick cooking spray. Add salmon. Grill for 5 minutes on each side. Remove from heat. Let stand, covered with foil, for 5 minutes. Cut into 4 pieces and serve.

Yield: 4 servings

Quick & Easy Grilling

Smoked Alaskan Salmon for a Crowd

30 pounds (about) salmon
1 (1-pound) package brown
    sugar
3/4 cup salt
2 tablespoons pepper

Clean, rinse and debone salmon; discard skin and bones. Cut into 1¹/2- to 2-inch pieces. Combine brown sugar, salt and pepper in bowl; mix well. Layer salmon and brown sugar mixture alternately in large plastic container until all ingredients are used. Let stand, covered, in cool dry place overnight. Prepare smoker using cottonwood or alder wood. Smoke salmon for 6 hours using manufacturer's directions.

Yield: 120 servings

Salmon with Tarragon Mayonnaise

2 cups mayonnaise
¹/4 cup chopped fresh tarragon
3 tablespoons minced green
    onions or red onion
2 tablespoons fresh lemon juice
2 tablespoons chopped capers
¹/4 teaspoon freshly ground
    pepper
Salt to taste
8 (4- to 6-ounce) salmon steaks

Blend the mayonnaise, tarragon, green onions, lemon juice, capers and pepper in a large bowl; season with salt. Chill, covered, for 2 to 24 hours. Place salmon on grill rack brushed with vegetable oil. Spread each steak with 2¹/2 tablespoons of tarragon mayonnaise mixture. Grill 5 inches above medium coals for 6 minutes. Turn salmon over and brush each steak with 2¹/2 tablespoons of tarragon mayonnaise mixture. Grill until salmon flakes easily and is barely opaque. Arrange salmon on serving platter. Garnish with halved lemon and lime slices and sprigs of fresh tarragon and parsley.

Yield: 8 servings

Quick & Easy Grilling

Grilled Salmon Steaks

1/2 cup (1 stick) margarine,
  melted
2 tablespoons lemon juice
1 tablespoon soy sauce
1 tablespoon parsley flakes
1 teaspoon garlic powder
1 teaspoon dill weed
1 teaspoon seasoned salt
1/4 teaspoon lemon pepper
  seasoning
6 (1-inch-thick) salmon steaks

Combine margarine, lemon juice, soy sauce, parsley, garlic powder, dill weed, seasoned salt and lemon pepper in bowl; mix well. Let stand for 15 to 20 minutes. Brush salmon with sauce. Spray grill with nonstick cooking spray. Grill over hot coals for 3 to 4 minutes on 1 side, basting once. Turn salmon. Grill for 3 to 4 minutes or until fish flakes easily, basting once. May substitute tuna for salmon.

Yield: 6 servings

Halibut Kabobs

1/2 cup olive oil
2 to 3 garlic cloves, minced
1 1/2 pounds halibut, cut into
  1 1/2-inch squares
3/4 cup Italian-flavored bread
  crumbs
4 slices bacon, cut into
  1 1/2-inch squares

Mix olive oil and garlic in bowl. Coat halibut with marinade. Roll halibut in bread crumbs. Alternate bacon pieces and halibut on skewers, beginning and ending with bacon pieces. Grill over medium coals, rotating every few minutes to ensure that bacon cooks without burning.

Yield: 4 servings

Quick & Easy Grilling

Grilled Trout in Foil

2 pounds trout
2 slices bacon
1 large onion, sliced
1 lemon, sliced
Lemon pepper to taste
Salt and black pepper to taste

Rinse trout and pat dry. Layer 1 bacon slice, half the onion slices and half the lemon slices on a large piece of heavy-duty foil. Place trout on top. Season with lemon pepper, salt and black pepper. Place remaining bacon slice, onion slices and lemon slices on top of trout. Fold foil to enclose and seal edges. Place on grill rack over hot coals. Grill for 10 minutes on each side. Trout should flake easily when done.

Yield: 4 servings

Bacon-Stuffed Trout

2 eggs
1 tablespoon milk
1 teaspoon parsley flakes
1 garlic clove, minced
1/2 teaspoon allspice
8 medium trout, cleaned
8 to 16 slices grilled bacon

Combine eggs, milk, parsley, garlic and allspice in bowl; beat well. Coat trout inside and out with egg mixture. Place 1 or 2 bacon slices in each trout. Place trout on hot greased grill. Grill over hot coals for 20 minutes or until trout flakes easily, turning once.

Yield: 8 servings

Quick & Easy Grilling

Zesty Grilled Tuna

3 tablespoons soy sauce
3 tablespoons orange juice
2 tablespoons ketchup
1 tablespoon vegetable oil
3/4 teaspoon chopped fresh
  parsley
1/2 shallot, chopped
1 garlic clove, minced
1 teaspoon lemon juice
1/2 teaspoon oregano
1/2 teaspoon pepper
1 pound tuna or swordfish fillets

Combine soy sauce, orange juice, ketchup, oil, parsley, shallot, garlic, lemon juice, oregano and pepper in a large bowl; mix well. Add tuna. Marinate at room temperature for 1 hour. Grill over medium coals for 4 to 6 minutes on each side or until firm.

Yield: 4 servings

Tuna with Mustard Marinade

2 tablespoons Dijon mustard
2 garlic cloves, minced
1/2 cup olive oil
Juice of 4 limes
1/4 cup soy sauce
1 teaspoon pepper
1 tablespoon chopped fresh
  dill weed
4 (1-inch) tuna steaks
Salt and pepper to taste
4 sprigs of fresh dill weed
4 lime slices
1 cup salsa

Combine Dijon mustard, garlic, olive oil, lime juice, soy sauce, 1 teaspoon pepper and 1 tablespoon dill weed in small bowl; mix well. Rub both sides of tuna with salt and pepper; place in large glass baking dish. Pour mustard marinade over tuna. Chill, covered, for 2 hours or longer, turning occasionally. Place tuna on grill rack. Grill 6 inches above medium coals for 4 to 6 minutes on each side or until firm, basting frequently with marinade. Garnish with dill weed sprigs and lime slices. Serve with salsa. May substitute Italian dressing for mustard marinade.

Yield: 4 servings

Quick & Easy Grilling

Grilled Tuna Burgers

1 cup mayonnaise
1 teaspoon toasted oriental
   sesame oil
1 teaspoon white wine vinegar
1/2 teaspoon cumin
2 drops of hot pepper sauce
1 tablespoon sesame seeds
2 cups shredded savoy cabbage
1 3/4 pounds tuna fillets, chilled
4 garlic cloves, minced
4 anchovies, minced
1/4 cup olive oil
1/4 cup chopped fresh basil
Salt and pepper to taste
Olive oil for sautéing
Burger buns, split, lightly toasted

Mix mayonnaise, sesame oil, vinegar, cumin, hot pepper sauce and sesame seeds in medium bowl. Add cabbage and toss to coat; set aside. Trim off any dark oily parts of tuna. Thinly slice tuna and chop until it is the texture of hamburger and presses into a compact ball. Mix in garlic, anchovies, olive oil, basil, salt and pepper. Divide mixture into 4 equal portions and shape into 1-inch-thick patties. Place patties 2 inches apart on grill rack coated with nonstick cooking spray. Grill over medium-hot coals for 1 minute per side for rare; 1 1/2 minutes for medium rare. Place burgers on 1 side of the split buns and top with sesame mayonnaise.

Yield: 4 servings

Oriental Grilled Tuna Steaks

6 (4-ounce) Alaskan tuna
   steaks, 3/4 inch thick
1 cup thinly sliced green onions
1/4 cup plus 2 tablespoons rice
   wine vinegar
1/4 cup plus 2 tablespoons low-
   sodium soy sauce
1 tablespoon sesame oil
1 tablespoon grated fresh
   gingerroot
1/4 teaspoon ground red pepper

Place tuna in shallow dish. Combine green onions, vinegar, soy sauce, sesame oil, gingerroot and red pepper in small bowl, stirring well. Reserve 1/4 of the mixture. Pour remaining mixture over the tuna. Refrigerate, covered, for 2 hours or longer. Spray grill rack with nonstick cooking spray. Grill tuna over medium coals for 4 minutes on each side or until firm, basting frequently with reserved green onion mixture.

Yield: 4 to 6 servings

Quick & Easy Grilling

Swordfish with Red Pepper Sauce

2 sprigs of rosemary, crushed
2 garlic cloves, minced
1/3 cup olive oil
2 tablespoons fresh lemon juice
1/2 teaspoon salt
1/2 teaspoon freshly ground
   pepper
4 (6-ounce) swordfish steaks
1 (12-ounce) jar roasted red
   bell peppers
1 tablespoon olive oil
1/3 cup reduced-sodium chicken
   broth
Salt and pepper to taste

Combine rosemary, garlic, 1/3 cup olive oil, lemon juice, salt and pepper in glass or nonreactive dish. Add swordfish, turning to coat. Chill, covered, for 2 to 8 hours. Pat bell peppers dry with paper towel. Combine bell peppers with 1 tablespoon olive oil and chicken broth in food processor. Season with salt and pepper to taste. Process with steel blade until puréed. Pour into saucepan. Simmer over low heat for 3 to 4 minutes to reduce liquid and blend flavors. Place swordfish on oiled grill rack or fish grill. Grill for 8 to 10 minutes or until swordfish flakes easily, turning once. Spoon equal amounts of warm pepper sauce onto 4 plates. Arrange swordfish over sauce. Serve immediately.

Yield: 4 servings

Scallops Grilled in Garlic Butter

1 cup (2 sticks) butter
2 large garlic cloves, cut into
   halves
Chopped onion to taste
2 tablespoons chopped fresh
   parsley
1/2 teaspoon tarragon
1/2 teaspoon salt
1/4 teaspoon pepper
2 pounds scallops

Melt butter in saucepan. Add garlic and cook over high heat until browned; remove with slotted spoon and discard. Add onion, parsley, tarragon, salt and pepper; mix well. Remove from heat. Rinse and drain scallops; place on large sheet of heavy-duty foil. Drizzle with seasoned butter. Fold foil to enclose and seal edges. Grill for 3 minutes on each side or until cooked through. May move closer to heat source during last minute of cooking time to brown if desired.

Yield: 6 servings

Quick & Easy Grilling

Grilled Shrimp-on-a-Stick

1 cup soy sauce
1/2 cup lemon juice
3 pounds large shrimp, peeled,
    deveined
Fresh mint leaves
1 pound bacon slices, cut into
    1-inch pieces
1/2 red bell pepper, cut into 11/2-
    inch pieces
1/2 yellow bell pepper, cut into
    11/2-inch pieces
Canned pineapple chunks

Combine soy sauce and lemon juice in shallow dish. Add shrimp and marinate for 1 to 2 hours. Fold mint leaves inside bacon. Thread shrimp, bacon, bell pepper pieces and pineapple chunks alternately onto skewers until all ingredients are used. Place on grill rack over hot coals. Grill until bacon is crisp, turning frequently.

Yield: 4 to 6 servings

Shrimp Fajitas

1 tablespoon safflower oil
1 tablespoon lime juice
11/2 teaspoons minced fresh
    oregano
1/4 teaspoon cumin
1 garlic clove, finely chopped
1 pound shrimp, peeled,
    deveined
8 flour tortillas, warmed
Salsa
Guacamole

Combine safflower oil, lime juice, oregano, cumin and garlic in bowl. Add shrimp and stir until coated. Chill, covered, for 30 minutes. Drain, reserving marinade. Thread shrimp onto skewers. Grill over medium coals for 4 to 5 minutes or until pink, turning and brushing with reserved marinade once. Discard remaining marinade. Place equal portions of shrimp on each tortilla. Add salsa and guacamole. Fold bottom edge of tortilla toward center; fold right and left sides over and top edge down. Serve with additional salsa and guacamole.

Yield: 8 servings

Quick & Easy Grilling

Ragin' Cajun Shrimp

4 pounds shrimp, peeled
1 cup corn oil
1/2 cup chopped green onions
2 garlic cloves, minced
1 teaspoon cayenne pepper
1 teaspoon black pepper
1/2 teaspoon red pepper flakes
1/2 teaspoon thyme
1/2 teaspoon rosemary
1/4 teaspoon oregano
Bamboo skewers

Combine shrimp, corn oil, green onions, garlic, cayenne pepper, black pepper, red pepper, thyme, rosemary and oregano in large bowl, stirring to coat shrimp. Refrigerate, covered, for 2 hours, stirring occasionally. Soak bamboo skewers in ice water for 2 hours. Drain shrimp, reserving marinade. Thread shrimp onto skewers. Grill just until pink, basting with marinade. Serve immediately.

Yield: 8 servings

Barbecued Shrimp

1/4 cup chopped onion
1/2 cup ketchup
2 tablespoons fresh rosemary,
    or 1 tablespoon dried
    rosemary
1 tablespoon brown sugar
1 tablespoon dry mustard
1 tablespoon white vinegar
1/4 teaspoon garlic powder
Hot sauce to taste
24 jumbo shrimp
1 lemon, cut into wedges

Heat nonstick skillet sprayed with nonstick cooking spray. Add onion. Sauté until tender; remove from heat. Stir in ketchup, rosemary, brown sugar, dry mustard, vinegar, garlic powder and hot sauce. Let stand for 2 to 3 hours. Peel and devein shrimp. Combine with marinade in shallow dish, turning to coat well. Marinate, covered, in refrigerator for 1 hour. Soak four 8-inch wooden skewers in water in bowl for 30 minutes; drain. Drain shrimp. Thread skewers through both ends of shrimp. Grill for 3 to 4 minutes on each side or until shrimp turn pink. Squeeze lemon juice over shrimp.

Yield: 4 servings

Quick & Easy Grilling

Shrimp and Chicken Kabobs

Wooden skewers
3/4 cup jalapeño jelly
2 tablespoons fresh lemon juice
36 jumbo shrimp
1 1/2 chicken breast fillets
1 pineapple
Salt and pepper to taste

Soak wooden skewers in water in bowl for 30 minutes. Combine jalapeño jelly and lemon juice in small saucepan. Heat over medium heat until jelly melts, stirring to mix well. Peel and devein shrimp, leaving tails. Cut chicken into 3/4-inch pieces. Cut pineapple into 3/4-inch pieces. Drain skewers. Thread shrimp, chicken and pineapple onto skewers. Place a few at a time in boiling salted water in deep skillet. Cook for 6 minutes; drain well. Brush with jelly mixture; season with salt and pepper. Place on oiled grill rack. Grill 5 to 6 inches above hot coals for 1 to 2 minutes or until golden brown, turning frequently.

Yield: 6 servings

Clam Bake in Foil

8 to 12 ounces chicken pieces
6 clams
1 pound fresh lobster, coarsely
    chopped
2 medium potatoes
2 small onions
2 small ears of corn
1/2 cup water

Rinse chicken and pat dry. Cut 2 large squares of heavy-duty foil. Divide chicken, clams, lobster, potatoes, onions, corn and water equally between each piece of foil. Seal foil packets securely. Grill over hot coals for 1 hour, turning packets frequently. Serve with melted butter and lemon wedges. May also include whole fresh green beans, Polish sausage, onions, mushrooms and/or shrimp.

Yield: 2 servings

Quick & Easy Grilling

Beginnings
& Endings

Hickory-Smoked Pineapple

2 cups hickory wood chips
1 cup ketchup
1/4 cup dark corn syrup
1 tablespoon Worcestershire
    sauce
1/8 teaspoon hot sauce
1 (15-ounce) can pineapple
    chunks, drained
1 pound sliced bacon
1 (11-ounce) can mandarin
    oranges, drained (optional)

Soak wood chips in water to cover in bowl for 30 minutes; drain. Mix ketchup, corn syrup, Worcestershire sauce and hot sauce in saucepan. Stir in pineapple chunks. Bring mixture to boil; reduce heat. Simmer for 10 minutes, stirring frequently. Cut bacon slices crosswise into halves. Drain pineapple, reserving sauce. Wrap each pineapple chunk with bacon slice and secure with wooden pick. Arrange on 2 large sheets of heavy-duty foil. Fold foil to enclose and seal edges. Prepare charcoal grill. Lay wet wood chips over red hot coals. Set foil package on grill. Smoke for 15 minutes. Baste with reserved sauce. Smoke for 15 minutes longer or until bacon is crisp. Skewer a mandarin orange slice to bottom of each pineapple chunk. Serve with remaining sauce.

Yield: 35 servings

Bacon-Wrapped Bananas

1 tablespoon honey
1/4 cup soy sauce
4 bananas, cut into large pieces
10 bacon slices, cut into halves

Blend honey and soy sauce in bowl. Pour marinade over bananas in bowl and stir lightly. Marinate bananas for about 30 minutes. Wrap bacon around each piece of banana and secure with wooden pick. Dip each in marinade and arrange on grill rack. Grill for 8 minutes or until bacon is crisp, turning once.

Yield: 20 pieces

Quick & Easy Grilling

Grilled Cheese Bread

5 ounces Romano cheese,
    grated
5 ounces Parmesan cheese,
    grated
1/2 teaspoon garlic powder
1 tablespoon minced onion
1 (8-ounce) jar mayonnaise
1 (16-ounce) loaf French bread,
    thinly sliced
Chopped fresh parsley to taste

Combine Romano cheese, Parmesan cheese, garlic powder and onion in bowl and mix well. Stir in mayonnaise. Spread bread slices with mixture. Arrange on grill rack. Sprinkle with parsley. Grill over medium coals until light brown and bubbly. Serve immediately.

Yield: 24 servings

Beef Jerky

1/4 cup Worcestershire sauce
1/4 cup soy sauce
2 tablespoons liquid smoke
1 teaspoon onion powder
1 teaspoon MSG
1/2 teaspoon seasoned salt
1/3 teaspoon garlic powder
1/4 teaspoon pepper
1 (1 1/2-pound) flank steak,
    cut into thin strips

Combine Worcestershire sauce, soy sauce, liquid smoke, onion powder, MSG, seasoned salt, garlic powder and pepper in glass dish or crock; mix well. Add steak, turning to coat. Marinate in refrigerator for 24 hours, turning occasionally; drain. Line grill rack with foil. Arrange steak strips on grill rack. Grill over low coals for 4 to 6 hours or to desired degree of dryness. Remove to wire rack to cool. Store in sealable plastic bags in refrigerator.

Yield: 48 servings

Quick & Easy Grilling

Parmesan Chicken Strips

*1 pound boneless skinless
    chicken breasts*
1/2 cup grated Parmesan cheese
*1/2 teaspoon chili powder or
    Hungarian paprika*
1 teaspoon oregano
1 teaspoon basil
1/4 teaspoon garlic powder
Salt and pepper to taste
2 eggs, beaten
Ranch salad dressing

Rinse chicken and pat dry. Cut into 1-inch-thick strips. Combine cheese, chili powder, oregano, basil, garlic powder, salt and pepper in shallow dish and mix well. Dip chicken in eggs; coat with cheese mixture. May double coat at this point, but increase amount of cheese and spices used. Arrange chicken strips on grill rack sprayed with nonstick cooking spray. Grill over medium coals for 18 to 20 minutes or until chicken is cooked through, turning once. Arrange on serving platter. Serve with ranch salad dressing.

Yield: 50 servings

Sesame Chicken Fingers

*8 ounces boneless skinless
    chicken breasts*
1 cup mayonnaise
2 teaspoons dried minced onion
2 teaspoons dry mustard
1 cup butter cracker crumbs
Sesame seeds to taste
1 cup mayonnaise
2 tablespoons honey

Rinse chicken and pat dry. Cut into 1/4-inch-thick strips. Combine 1 cup mayonnaise, onion and dry mustard in bowl and mix well. Combine cracker crumbs and sesame seeds in bowl and mix well. Dip chicken strips into mayonnaise mixture; coat with cracker crumb mixture. Arrange strips in a single layer on grill rack sprayed with nonstick cooking spray. Grill over medium coals for 18 to 20 minutes or until chicken is cooked through, turning once. Arrange on serving platter. Serve with mixture of 1 cup mayonnaise and honey.

Yield: 10 to 12 servings

Quick & Easy Grilling

Grilled Potato Salad

3 pounds red boiling potatoes
1/3 cup olive oil
1 garlic clove
1/4 cup red wine vinegar
1 tablespoon fresh rosemary, or
    1 teaspoon dried rosemary
Salt to taste
1/3 cup olive oil
2 pounds green beans, cut into
    1-inch pieces
1 red onion
30 kalamata or niçoise olives,
    cut into halves

Cut unpeeled potatoes into halves and then into 1-inch wedges. Combine with 1/3 cup olive oil in large bowl, tossing to coat well. Arrange in single layer on heavy-duty foil. Fold foil to enclose and seal edges. Place on grill rack and grill over medium coals for 30 minutes or until tender, stirring every 10 minutes. Remove from grill and cool. Process garlic, vinegar, rosemary, salt and 1/3 cup olive oil in blender until smooth. Cook beans in salted water in saucepan for 5 minutes or until tender-crisp; drain. Cut onion into halves lengthwise and then into thin slices. Crisp in ice water for 5 minutes; drain and pat dry. Combine potatoes, beans, onion, olives and dressing in bowl; toss lightly to coat well. Garnish with sprigs of fresh rosemary.

Yield: 10 servings

Mango and Red Onion Salad

2 red bell peppers
2 red onions, sliced crosswise
    about 1/4 inch thick
2 ripe mangoes
1 small bunch cilantro
3 tablespoons olive oil
1 tablespoon lime juice
Salt and freshly cracked black
    pepper
4 small bunches arugula

Roast bell peppers over grill until skins are dark and blistered. Place in a paper or plastic food storage bag; close top. Set aside for 5 to 10 minutes; peel. Remove skins under running water. Cut into quarters; remove seeds and stem. Grill onions until lightly browned. Cut mangoes into thick slices. Combine peppers, onions and mango slices in bowl. Add sprigs of cilantro. Add olive oil, lime juice, salt and pepper to taste. Arrange arugula on 4 salad plates; top with mango mixture.

Yield: 4 servings

Quick & Easy Grilling

Grilled Eggplant Salad

2 small eggplant
Salt to taste
1 cup olive oil
3 tomatoes, sliced
1 cup (4 ounces) shredded
    mozzarella cheese
1/2 cup kalamata olives
2 tablespoons capers
Green olive oil to taste
Red wine vinegar to taste
Freshly ground pepper to taste
5 basil leaves, julienned

Peel eggplant under running water; cut into 1-inch slices. Sprinkle with salt. Let stand in colander for 20 minutes. Rinse eggplant and pat dry. Place in shallow dish. Pour 1 cup olive oil over eggplant, tossing to coat. Let stand for 10 minutes; drain. Grill over hot coals until brown on both sides. Layer eggplant and tomato slices on serving platter. Sprinkle with cheese, olives and capers. Drizzle with green olive oil and vinegar. Season with salt and pepper; top with basil. Substitute roasted red bell peppers for tomatoes in winter. May prepare eggplant 3 hours before serving.

Yield: 4 servings

Grilled Summer Salad

1/4 cup balsamic vinegar or
    lemon juice
2 tablespoons olive oil
2 tablespoons water
1/2 tablespoon chopped fresh
    basil or parsley
1 garlic clove, minced
1 Vidalia or sweet onion, sliced
1 tomato, sliced
1 pineapple, sliced
1 squash or zucchini, sliced
8 ounces mixed salad greens
Salt and pepper to taste

Whisk vinegar, olive oil, water, basil and garlic in small bowl. Arrange onion, tomato, pineapple and squash in large shallow dish. Pour marinade mixture over vegetable mixture and let stand for 30 to 60 minutes. Drain, reserving marinade. Grill vegetable mixture over medium hot coals for 2 to 3 minutes on each side. Drizzle reserved marinade over salad greens. Top with grilled vegetable mixture. Season with salt and pepper.

Yield: 2 to 4 servings

Quick & Easy Grilling

Thai Beef Salad

1 (1-pound) 1¹/2- to 2-inch-thick
    top sirloin steak
Salt to taste
1 small serrano chile, stemmed
2 garlic cloves, peeled, stemmed
¹/4 cup soy sauce
1 minced anchovy
Zest of 2 large limes
Juice of 2 large limes
1 tablespoon brown sugar
¹/2 cup peanut oil
1 teaspoon ginger
¹/2 cup lightly packed chopped
    fresh mint leaves
4 shallots, sliced lengthwise
¹/4 cup chopped green onions
Mixed salad greens

Place steak on work surface. Salt lightly. Grill over hot coals for 2 to 3 minutes on each side or until rare to medium-rare. Transfer to rack. Let cool to room temperature. Purée serrano chile, garlic, soy sauce and anchovy in blender or food processor. Add lime zest, lime juice and brown sugar. Process again. Divide into 2 bowls. Whisk peanut oil into mixture in 1 bowl; reserve for salad dressing. Whisk ginger, mint, shallots and green onions into mixture in remaining bowl. Carve steak on diagonal into ¹/4-inch slices. Cut slices into ¹/4-inch strips; discard any fat. Toss steak with mint sauce in bowl. Cover and refrigerate. Place salad greens in large bowl. Cover and refrigerate. Toss greens with ¹/2 cup reserved salad dressing. Toss meat strips several times. Place in center of greens.

Yield: 4 to 6 servings

Sirloin Steak Salad

1¹/2 pounds boneless sirloin steak
Garlic powder, pepper and
    seasoned salt to taste
1 envelope ranch salad
    dressing mix
1 cup mayonnaise
1 cup sour cream
1 pint cherry tomatoes, quartered
4 ounces fresh mushrooms, sliced

Season steak with garlic powder, pepper and seasoned salt. Grill over hot coals until steak is done to taste. Chill in refrigerator; trim. Slice thinly cross grain. Combine salad dressing mix, mayonnaise and sour cream in bowl; mix well. Chill in refrigerator. Toss steak with enough dressing to coat. Add tomatoes and mushrooms. Add additional dressing if necessary.

Yield: 4 servings

Quick & Easy Grilling

Grilled Chicken and Red Pepper Pasta Salad

16 ounces bow tie pasta,
  cooked, drained
1 (12-ounce) jar marinated
  artichoke hearts
1/3 cup sliced black olives
1 (28-ounce) jar chunky
  spaghetti sauce
1/2 cup olive oil
2 tablespoons wine vinegar
2 tablespoons minced fresh
  parsley
1/2 teaspoon salt
2 red bell peppers, halved
  lengthwise, seeded
Olive oil to taste
Salt and pepper to taste
1 pound boneless skinless
  chicken breasts
1 tablespoon toasted pine nuts
  (optional)

Combine pasta, artichokes, olives, spaghetti sauce, 1/2 cup olive oil, vinegar, parsley and 1/2 teaspoon salt in large bowl and mix well. Chill, covered. Brush bell peppers with olive oil and season with salt and pepper. Place bell peppers and chicken on grill rack and grill over medium-hot coals for 5 to 6 minutes on each side or until bell peppers are browned and chicken is cooked through. Remove from heat and let stand until cool enough to handle. Thinly slice bell peppers and chicken and serve over pasta salad. Garnish with pine nuts.

Yield: 6 to 8 servings

Quick & Easy Grilling

Grilled Chicken Caesar Salad

2 large garlic bulbs
1/4 cup white wine vinegar
1 tablespoon olive oil
Pepper to taste
1 tablespoon red wine vinegar
2 tablespoons fresh lemon juice
1 teaspoon Dijon mustard
1 tablespoon anchovy paste
1 teaspoon Worcestershire sauce
Dash of Tabasco sauce
1/3 cup olive oil
2 large heads romaine
1 1/4 cups grated Parmesan
   cheese
3 cups garlic herb croutons
4 boneless skinless chicken
   breasts, grilled, sliced

Peel off papery outer skin of garlic, leaving bulbs intact; place in small baking dish. Pour white wine vinegar over garlic. Drizzle with 1 tablespoon olive oil. Season with pepper. Bake, covered with foil, at 300 degrees for 1 1/2 hours or until garlic is very soft like paste. Let stand until cool. Squeeze garlic to remove cloves from skins; place in small bowl. Mash with a fork to form paste; place in blender. Add red wine vinegar, lemon juice, Dijon mustard, anchovy paste, Worcestershire sauce and Tabasco sauce. Add 1/3 cup olive oil in a fine stream, processing constantly at high speed until smooth. May prepare up to 2 hours before serving. Let stand at room temperature. Tear romaine into bite-size pieces; place in salad bowl. Pour in dressing, tossing to mix. Add cheese and croutons; toss to mix. Arrange chicken slices over salad. Season with pepper. Serve immediately. May top with large grilled shrimp or slices of grilled beef tenderloin.

Yield: 8 servings

Quick & Easy Grilling

Grilled Vegetable Hoagies

1 zucchini
1 yellow squash
2 Roma tomatoes
1 small eggplant
6 large white mushrooms
1/4 cup low-fat Italian salad
    dressing
4 (6-inch) French rolls
1/2 cup (2 ounces) shredded
    low-fat mozzarella cheese
Basil

Slice vegetables into thin strips; pat dry. Grill crisscross marks on each strip. Drizzle with salad dressing. Place vegetables on split French rolls. Top with cheese. Toast in a 400-degree oven until brown. Top with basil.

Yield: 4 servings

Pizza on the Grill

8 ounces pizza cheese, shredded
2 large Roma tomatoes, sliced
1/2 to 1 jalapeño chile, finely
    chopped (optional)
2 1/2 tablespoons chopped fresh
    cilantro or parsley
1 (12-inch) unbaked pizza crust

Layer cheese, tomatoes, jalapeño chile and cilantro on pizza crust. Place on grill rack. Lower grill lid. Grill pizza 4 to 6 inches above medium coals for 8 minutes or until crust is crisp and cheese is melted. Slip a piece of foil under pizza if crust is browning too fast.

Yield: 8 servings

Quick & Easy Grilling

Zesty Horseradish Corn on Cob

1/2 cup (1 stick) margarine,
    softened
1/2 teaspoon salt
1/4 teaspoon pepper
1 tablespoon chopped fresh
    parsley
2 tablespoons country-style
    Dijon mustard
2 teaspoons horseradish
8 fresh ears of corn, shucked

Combine margarine, salt, pepper, parsley, Dijon mustard and horseradish in small bowl; mix well. Spread 1 tablespoon mixture evenly over each ear of corn. Wrap tightly in heavy-duty foil. Grill over hot coals for 15 to 20 minutes, turning several times.

Yield: 8 servings

Parmesan Grilled Corn

1/2 cup (1 stick) butter, softened
1/4 cup grated Parmesan cheese
1/4 cup mayonnaise
1 tablespoon instant minced
    onion
1/4 teaspoon garlic powder
1/4 teaspoon white pepper
1 or 2 ears of corn per person

Combine butter, cheese, mayonnaise, onion, garlic powder and white pepper in mixing bowl. Beat for 2 to 3 minutes or until light and creamy. Chill, covered, for 1 hour or longer. Spread corn generously with butter mixture. Wrap ears individually in foil. Place on grill over low coals. Grill for 20 minutes, turning frequently.

Yield: variable

Quick & Easy Grilling

Italian Eggplant Stacks

6 (1/4-inch) slices eggplant

2 teaspoons olive oil

1/3 cup plus 2 teaspoons
    part-skim ricotta cheese

1/2 ounce cooked smoked ham,
    chopped

2 tablespoons chopped fresh
    basil, or 1/2 teaspoon dried
    basil

1/8 teaspoon pepper

6 tomato slices

2 ounces mozzarella cheese,
    shredded

Arrange eggplant slices on grill rack sprayed with nonstick cooking spray. Brush eggplant with 1 teaspoon of olive oil. Grill 5 to 6 inches above hot coals for 2 to 3 minutes or until light brown; turn slices. Brush with remaining olive oil. Grill for 2 to 3 minutes longer or until light brown. Combine ricotta cheese, ham, basil and pepper in bowl; mix well. Spread equal amounts of cheese mixture on eggplant slices; top with tomato slices. Sprinkle with shredded mozzarella cheese. Broil for 2 to 3 minutes or until cheese melts. Let stand for 2 to 3 minutes before serving.

Yield: 2 servings

Eggplant and Squash

1/2 cup canola oil

1/4 cup light olive oil

1/4 cup lemon juice

1 teaspoon oregano

1 teaspoon salt

1/2 teaspoon garlic powder

1/4 teaspoon pepper

1 large or 2 small eggplant,
    cut into 1/2-inch slices

4 yellow squash, cut into
    1/2-inch slices

4 zucchini, cut into 1/2-inch
    slices

Combine canola oil, olive oil, lemon juice, oregano, salt, garlic powder and pepper in bowl and mix well. Dip eggplant, squash and zucchini in oil mixture; drain slightly. Grill over medium-hot coals for 8 to 10 minutes per side or until brown. Serve immediately or cover to keep warm.

Yield: 5 servings

Quick & Easy Grilling

Grilled Mushrooms with Bacon

24 large whole mushrooms
24 slices bacon
1 cup (2 sticks) margarine,
    melted
1 cup teriyaki sauce
1/4 cup liquid smoke
1/4 cup packed dark brown
    sugar
1/4 teaspoon onion powder
1/4 teaspoon garlic powder

Wrap each mushroom with bacon slice, securing end with wooden pick. Combine margarine, teriyaki sauce, liquid smoke, brown sugar, onion powder and garlic powder in bowl; mix well. Place mushrooms in 9×13-inch baking pan. Pour marinade over mushrooms. Grill over medium-hot coals for 30 minutes or until bacon is done, basting occasionally with marinade.

Yield: 8 to 10 servings

Grilled Shiitake Mushrooms

16 medium shiitake mushrooms
2 tablespoons chopped garlic
1/4 to 1/2 cup olive oil
1 tablespoon chopped fresh
    parsley
2 teaspoons thyme
Salt and pepper to taste

Combine mushrooms with garlic, olive oil, parsley, thyme, salt and pepper in small bowl; mix gently. Marinate for 20 minutes. Grill mushrooms for 8 to 10 minutes.

Yield: 4 servings

Quick & Easy Grilling

Honey-Grilled Onions

3 large red onions
1/4 cup water
1/3 cup honey
3 tablespoons butter or
    margarine, melted
1 teaspoon paprika
1 teaspoon coriander
1/2 teaspoon salt
1/8 teaspoon cayenne pepper

Peel and cut each onion into halves horizontally. Arrange onions cut side down on grill rack. Sprinkle with water. Grill, covered with foil, over medium hot coals for 30 minutes. Mix honey, butter, paprika, coriander, salt and cayenne pepper in bowl. Remove onions from oven, turn cut side up and spoon half glaze mixture over them. Return to grill. Grill, uncovered, for 15 minutes. Baste with remaining glaze. Grill for an additional 15 to 20 minutes or until onions are tender. Serve hot or at room temperature.

Yield: 6 servings

Barbecued Onions

1/2 cup cider vinegar
1/2 cup white vinegar
2/3 cup vegetable oil
2 teaspoons Worcestershire
    sauce
2 to 3 garlic cloves, minced
1/2 teaspoon paprika
3 tablespoons ketchup
1/2 teaspoon dry mustard
Tabasco sauce to taste
6 large Vidalia onions, sliced

Process cider vinegar, white vinegar, oil, Worcestershire sauce, garlic, paprika, ketchup, dry mustard and Tabasco sauce in blender until smooth. Pour marinade over onion slices in shallow dish. Cover and refrigerate for 6 to 8 hours. Place onions with a small amount of marinade in foil and grill over low coals for 30 minutes.

Yield: 10 servings

Quick & Easy Grilling

Dilly Taters

4 red potatoes
1 green bell pepper
1/2 large onion, chopped
1 tablespoon margarine, melted
2 teaspoons dill seasoning
1 tablespoon water

Cut potatoes into quarters. Slice bell pepper into 1-inch pieces. Layer potatoes, bell pepper and onion on large piece of foil. Drizzle with margarine; sprinkle with dill seasoning and water. Fold the foil to enclose and seal edges. Grill over medium-hot coals for 10 minutes on each side or until potatoes are done.

Yield: 4 servings

Potatoes-on-a-Stick

Red potatoes and yams
1/4 cup olive oil
1/4 cup canola oil
2 to 4 tablespoons margarine, melted
3 tablespoons chopped fresh parsley
1 tablespoon chopped fresh tarragon
1/3 teaspoon crushed red pepper
1/2 teaspoon black pepper
1/2 teaspoon salt

Scrub desired number of potatoes and yams. Steam in steamer in saucepan for 20 minutes or just until tender. Drain; cool in cold water. Drain and pat dry. Combine olive oil, canola oil, margarine, parsley, tarragon, red pepper, black pepper and salt in large bowl. Cut potatoes and yams into 1 1/2-inch chunks; dip in olive oil mixture and thread onto skewers. Grill over hot coals until skins are brown and crusty, basting frequently with remaining olive oil mixture. Delicious for a fish cookout.

Yield: variable

Quick & Easy Grilling

Grilled New Potato Casserole

6 large new potatoes, sliced
1 red bell pepper, chopped
1 large Vidalia or other sweet
    onion, chopped
6 to 8 slices prosciutto, cut into
    1-inch pieces
1 to 2 tablespoons olive oil
1 teaspoon herbed garlic salt or
    salt, pepper and rosemary
    to taste

Place potatoes, bell pepper, onion and prosciutto on a large piece of heavy-duty foil. Drizzle with olive oil and sprinkle with garlic salt. Toss to coat. Fold foil to enclose and seal edges. Grill over medium coals for 45 minutes or until onion is browned and potatoes are tender, stirring occasionally. Serve with grilled meats in summer or pheasant in winter.

Yield: 6 servings

Gingered Acorn Squash

2 small acorn squash
1/4 cup fresh orange juice
1/2 teaspoon ginger
1/2 teaspoon nutmeg

Cut squash into halves; remove and discard seeds. Cut a thin slice from bottom of squash so each half will stand straight. Arrange squash on grill rack. Place 1 tablespoon orange juice in cavity of each squash. Sprinkle with ginger and nutmeg. Cover with foil. Grill over medium coals for 1 to 1 1/2 hours or until tender. Let stand for 5 minutes before serving.

Yield: 4 servings

Quick & Easy Grilling

Jiffy Tomato Stack-Ups

1 (10-ounce) package frozen
    chopped broccoli
1 cup (4 ounces) shredded
    Swiss cheese
1/4 cup finely chopped onion
4 large tomatoes

Cook broccoli using package directions; drain. Combine broccoli, cheese and onion in bowl. Cut tomatoes into 1/2-inch-thick slices and place on large piece of heavy-duty foil. Top each tomato slice with broccoli mixture. Fold foil to enclose and seal edges. Grill 3 to 5 inches from hot coals for 8 minutes or until cheese melts.

Yield: 4 servings

Grilled Tomatoes

4 medium tomatoes, cut into
    halves horizontally
1/2 cup bread crumbs
1/4 cup (1/2 stick) butter or
    margarine, melted
3 small garlic cloves, crushed
3 tablespoons chopped green
    onions
2 tablespoons chopped fresh
    flat-leaf parsley
1 teaspoon basil

Arrange tomatoes on large piece of heavy-duty foil. Combine bread crumbs, butter, garlic, green onions, parsley and basil in bowl and mix well. Spread tomatoes with bread crumb mixture. Fold foil to enclose and seal edges. Chill for up to 5 hours. Let stand until room temperature. Place tomatoes on grill rack. Grill over hot coals until light brown.

Yield: 8 servings

Quick & Easy Grilling

Grilled Zucchini

2 medium zucchini
1/4 cup olive oil
1/4 cup balsamic vinegar
Salt and pepper to taste

Cut zucchini into halves lengthwise. Pour mixture of olive oil, vinegar, salt and pepper into shallow glass dish. Place zucchini cut side down in olive oil mixture. Marinate at room temperature for 1 hour, turning once. Grill over hot coals until tender, turning once; baste frequently.

Yield: 4 servings

Grilled Ratatouille

1 eggplant, sliced, salted
2 green bell peppers, cut into
   1/2-inch slices
2 small zucchini, sliced
1 onion, chopped
4 plum tomatoes, quartered
3 large garlic cloves
1/4 cup vegetable oil
1/2 teaspoon oregano
1 tablespoon chopped fresh
   basil
1/2 teaspoon salt
1/4 teaspoon coarsely ground
   pepper

Combine eggplant, bell peppers, zucchini, onion, tomatoes, garlic, oil, oregano, basil, salt and pepper in cast-iron skillet and mix well. Place skillet on grill over medium coals. Cook with grill lid closed for 25 minutes, stirring mixture once after 10 minutes.

Yield: 4 servings

Quick & Easy Grilling

Grilled Vegetable Kabobs

1/2 cup oil-free Italian salad
   dressing
1 tablespoon minced parsley
1 teaspoon basil
2 medium yellow squash, cut
   into 1-inch pieces
8 small onions
8 cherry tomatoes
8 medium mushrooms
2 cups cooked long grain rice

Combine salad dressing, parsley and basil in small bowl. Chill, covered, in refrigerator. Alternate squash, onions, tomatoes and mushrooms on 8 skewers. Place on grill rack sprayed with nonstick cooking spray. Grill over medium coals for 15 minutes or until vegetables are tender, basting frequently with salad dressing mixture. Place 1/2 cup rice on each serving plate; top each with 2 vegetable kabobs.

Yield: 4 servings

Foil-Grilled Vegetables

3 or 4 Roma tomatoes, cut into
   quarters
1 large onion, sliced
2 small zucchini, sliced
Florets of 1/2 bunch broccoli
Florets of 1/3 head cauliflower
1 tablespoon brown sugar
Sweet basil to taste
1 teaspoon instant beef bouillon
2 tablespoons margarine

Combine tomatoes, onion, zucchini, broccoli and cauliflower in bowl; mix gently. Sprinkle with brown sugar, basil and bouillon; toss gently to mix. Spread vegetables on large sheet of heavy-duty foil. Dot with margarine. Fold foil to enclose and seal edges. Grill over hot coals for 12 to 15 minutes or until tender. Serve hot.

Yield: 4 to 6 servings

Quick & Easy Grilling

Fruit Kabobs on the Grill

3 tablespoons butter or
    margarine, melted
1/2 cup apricot preserves or jam
1 teaspoon curry powder
Fresh peaches, pineapples,
    strawberries, bananas,
    apples, melons and oranges

Mix butter, preserves and curry powder in bowl. Coat fruit with sauce. Thread onto skewers. Grill over medium coals until heated through, basting with sauce and turning often.

Yield: variable

Grilled Pear and Banana Kabobs

2 pears, peeled, cut into chunks
2 bananas, peeled, cut into
    chunks
16 large strawberries, hulled
Juice of 2 lemons
3 tablespoons sugar

Combine pears, bananas and strawberries in bowl. Sprinkle with lemon juice and 1 1/2 tablespoons sugar. Let stand for 30 minutes. Thread onto skewers; coat with remaining sugar. Grill over medium coals for 5 to 6 minutes or until sugar caramelizes.

Yield: 4 servings

Barbecued Apples

4 small Granny Smith apples
1/4 cup packed dark brown
    sugar
2 tablespoons raisins
1 teaspoon grated lemon rind
1/2 teaspoon cinnamon

Core and cut ring around each apple with knife. Mix brown sugar, raisins, lemon rind and cinnamon in small bowl. Spoon mixture into cored centers. Wrap each apple in heavy-duty foil with shiny side against apple. Grill over warm coals for 40 minutes, turning occasionally. Unwrap carefully to serve.

Yield: 4 servings

Quick & Easy Grilling

Caramelized Apricot Apple Kabobs

12 ripe apricots, cut into halves
Juice of 1 orange
2 tart apples, peeled, cut into
    chunks
Juice of 1 lemon
12 large grapes
2 tablespoons sugar

Combine apricots and orange juice in bowl. Combine apples and lemon juice in separate bowl. Let stand for 30 minutes. Thread apricots, apples and grapes onto skewers. Coat with sugar. Grill over medium-hot coals for 5 to 6 minutes or until sugar caramelizes.

Yield: 4 servings

Bananas Foster on the Grill

1/4 cup molasses
1 tablespoon pineapple juice
1 teaspoon almond extract
1/4 cup (1/2 stick) butter
1/2 cup packed brown sugar
Cinnamon and nutmeg to taste
1 teaspoon lemon juice
1/2 teaspoon vanilla extract
6 firm bananas

Combine molasses, pineapple juice and almond extract in small bowl and mix well; set aside. Bring butter, brown sugar, cinnamon and nutmeg to a boil in small heavy saucepan. Reduce heat and simmer for 5 minutes or until slightly thickened, stirring constantly. Remove from heat. Stir in molasses mixture, lemon juice and vanilla. Cut a slit lengthwise in peel of each banana, leaving peel intact. Loosen peel gently from banana with tip of knife. Spoon some of molasses sauce into each slit and pat peel into place. Grill, covered, for 2 minutes. Spoon molasses sauce into banana peels every 2 minutes for 8 to 10 minutes or until bananas are tender and sauce is bubbly. Serve bananas with a scoop of vanilla ice cream.

Yield: 6 servings

Quick & Easy Grilling

Grilled Banana Split

1 banana
2 tablespoons honey
4 large strawberries
1/2 cup pineapple chunks
1 scoop nonfat frozen yogurt
Fat-free chocolate sauce
Fat-free granola
Fresh mint leaves

Cut unpeeled banana into halves lengthwise. Drizzle with honey. Grill for 2 minutes on each side. Peel; place in dessert bowl. Thread strawberries and pineapple chunks onto skewers. Grill for 1 to 2 minutes, turning once. Spread frozen yogurt on banana. Drizzle with chocolate sauce. Sprinkle with granola. Top with grilled strawberries and pineapple and fresh mint leaves.

Yield: 1 serving

Grilled Peaches Flambé

8 peach halves
1/2 cup packed light brown
   sugar
1 tablespoon butter or
   margarine
Sugar cubes
Lemon extract
Ice cream

Arrange peach halves cut side up on a piece of heavy-duty foil. Place 1 tablespoon brown sugar and 1 dot of butter in center of each. Fold foil to enclose and seal edges. Grill 3 inches from hot coals until sugar melts and peaches are heated through. Dissolve sugar cubes in lemon extract in saucepan. Heat over low heat. Spoon ice cream into serving dishes. Pour lemon mixture over peaches; ignite. Spoon over ice cream. Serve immediately.

Yield: 8 servings

Quick & Easy Grilling

Grilled Peaches with Raspberry Purée

1/2 (10-ounce) package frozen
  raspberries in light syrup,
  slightly thawed
1 1/2 teaspoons lemon juice
2 medium peaches, peeled, cut
  into halves
1 1/2 tablespoons light brown
  sugar
1/4 teaspoon cinnamon
1 1/2 teaspoons vanilla extract
1 1/2 teaspoons margarine

Process raspberries and lemon juice in blender until smooth. Strain into small bowl. Chill, covered, in refrigerator. Place peach halves cut side up on 18-inch square piece of foil. Fill centers with mixture of brown sugar and cinnamon. Sprinkle with vanilla; dot with margarine. Fold foil to enclose and seal edges. Grill over medium coals 15 minutes or until heated through. Place peaches on serving plates; spoon raspberry purée into centers.

Yield: 4 servings

Honey-Grilled Peaches

1/2 cup packed brown sugar
1/2 cup chopped pecans
Cinnamon to taste
1/4 cup (1/2 stick) butter, melted
2 tablespoons honey
4 firm peaches, peeled, halved

Mix brown sugar, pecans and cinnamon in bowl and set aside. Combine butter and honey in small bowl. Brush over peaches. Place peaches cut side down on grill. Grill until cut sides are golden brown, brushing with honey mixture. Turn peaches right side up and spoon pecan mixture into cavities. Grill just until peaches are tender and brown sugar is melted. Serve with ice cream if desired.

Yield: 8 servings

Quick & Easy Grilling

Paradise Grilled Papaya

1 papaya
1/4 cup lime juice
1/2 cup (1 stick) butter, melted
1 tablespoon honey

Peel papaya and cut into wedges, discarding seeds. Combine lime juice, butter and honey in bowl and mix well. Brush papaya with lime juice mixture and place in grill basket. Grill just until papaya is golden brown, turning occasionally and basting with lime juice mixture. Serve with remaining lime mixture.

Yield: 4 servings

Grilled Pineapple

2 ripe pineapples, peeled, cut
    into 1-inch slices
1 cup packed brown sugar

Arrange pineapple in shallow dish; sprinkle with brown sugar. Let stand for 1 hour or longer. Brush excess brown sugar from pineapple and place on grill rack. Grill over warm coals until brown on both sides, turning occasionally. Serve alone or with vanilla ice cream.

Yield: 10 to 12 servings

Grilled S'mores

9 large marshmallows
18 graham crackers
3 (2-ounce) milk chocolate
    candy bars, broken
    into thirds

Thread marshmallows onto skewers. Place skewers on grill rack and grill over hot coals, turning until marshmallows are brown and crispy. Layer 9 graham crackers with chocolate and marshmallows; top with remaining graham crackers and press together gently.

Yield: 9 servings

Quick & Easy Grilling

INDEX

Quick & Easy Grilling

Quick & Easy Grilling

Quick & Easy Grilling

Quick & Easy Grilling